STRENGTHEN THE COUNTRY
AND
ENRICH THE PEOPLE

Strengthen the Country
and
Enrich the People

The Reform Writings of Ma Jianzhong (1845-1900)

Translated & Introduced by
PAUL J. BAILEY

Durham East Asia Series
No.2

Routledge
Taylor & Francis Group

LONDON AND NEW YORK

STRENGTHEN THE COUNTRY
AND ENRICH THE PEOPLE

First published 1998 by
CURZON PRESS LTD

2 Park Square, Milton Park, Abingdon, Oxon OX14 4RN
711 Third Avenue, New York, NY 10017, USA

Routledge is an imprint of the Taylor & Francis Group, an informa business

First issued in paperback 2016

British Library Cataloguing in Publication Data
A CIP catologue entry for this book
is available from the British Library

ISBN 978-1-138-98301-4 (pbk)
ISBN 978-0-7007-0468-2 (hbk)

Typeset by Bookman, Slough, in Bembo 12 on 13pt.

Contents

The text of Ma's writings that I have used is the one published in Beijing in 1960, entitled *Shike jiyan* (Recorded words from the Shike Studio), and used on the jacket of this book.

ACKNOWLEDGEMENTS
I would like to thank my graduate student, Zhang Ming, for her invaluable assistance. I would also like to thank the ADM Faculty Group of the University of Edinburgh for providing research funds.

PAUL BAILEY

Introduction

THE SELF-STRENGTHENING MOVEMENT

C hina's modernization effort in the latter half of the nineteenth century has long been a lively topic of debate amongst historians. Initiated in response to a wave of domestic rebellions that threatened the survival of the ruling Qing dynasty (1644-1912) from the 1850s to the 1870s,[1] this modernization effort also sought to strengthen the country's defences in the wake of continued foreign encroachment first demonstrated by the Treaty of Nanjing (1842) ending the Anglo-Chinese Opium War. Often referred to generally as the Self-Strengthening Movement,[2] it began in the early 1860s at a time when the dynasty was attempting finally to crush the largest of the domestic rebellions, that of the *Taiping Tianguo* (Heavenly Kingdom of Great Peace), while also adjusting to the consequences of further treaties (in 1858 and 1860) imposed on China by Britain and France; these treaties created additional treaty ports in which foreigners could reside, trade and enjoy the privilege of extraterritoriality, opened up the Yangzi river to foreign shipping, provided for a permanent foreign diplomatic presence in Beijing, and allowed Western missionaries to travel, reside and proseletyze in the interior beyond the treaty ports.[3]

In addition to promoting traditional ideals of Confucian government, particularly in those areas devastated by internal rebellion, such as reducing the burden of land taxation, ensuring the efficacy of public works, and guarding against official corruption– all to be guaranteed by the morally upright official concerned with 'securing the people's livelihood' (*an minsheng*)– the court sanctioned a number of institutional and military measures with the aim of combatting future external and internal threats. In 1861 a government office (the *Zongli Yamen*) was created to oversee relations with the Western powers and in the following year an interpreters' college (the *Tongwenguan*) was opened to train diplomatic personnel. In 1863 and 1864 foreign language schools were also established in Shanghai and Guangzhou respectively. At the same time prominent provincial officials involved in the suppression of domestic rebellion also began to establish arsenals for the manufacture of Western-style armaments, the largest of which were those in Shanghai (1865), Nanjing (1867), Tianjin (1867) and Lanzhou (1871). In 1866 China's first modern naval dockyard (with an attached training school) was opened in Fuzhou.

Over the course of the next two decades the scope of the modernization process widened, beginning with the creation in 1872 of the first major officially-sponsored merchant enterprise, the China Merchants' Steam Navigation Company. Officials such as Li Hongzhang (1823-1901) increasingly emphasized the importance of economic development, and championed the exploitation of mineral resources, the building of railroads and telegraph lines, and the creation of modern manufacturing industry. Modern coal mining activity began in 1876 with the opening of the Keelung mine in Taiwan, to be followed a year later by the opening of the Kaiping mine in north China. By 1879 a telegraph line linked Tianjin with Dagu and in 1881 China's first railroad began operating from the Kaiping coal mine. In 1882, after several years planning, the Shanghai Cotton Cloth Mill was officially established to produce machine-manufactured cloth and yarn. On the eve of the Sino-Japanese War (1894-95) another prominent official,

Zhang Zhidong (1837-1909), was planning the formation of an industrial complex in the central province of Hubei linking a previously established (in 1890) ironworks and coal mine with new steel mills. These decades also witnessed an expansion of educational and training programmes. Between 1872 and 1881 Chinese students were sent to the US, army officers were sent to Germany in 1876 for training and in 1877 graduates from the Fuzhou Dockyard Naval School were sent to France and Britain for further training. Army and navy academies were opened in Tianjin (1885) and Nanjing (1890) respectively.[4]

Finally, from the mid-1870s, China embarked on a more active diplomatic policy with the posting of its official representatives abroad. Such a policy originated with a radical new approach to overseas Chinese who had emigrated to Southeast Asia and the Americas. In contrast to previous official attitudes that had equated overseas Chinese with rebels, pirates and traitors who had 'deserted' the embrace of China's civilization, Qing dynasty officials after the 1870s showed increasing concern for the plight of their compatriots, particularly that of indentured labourers often recruited illegally by Westerners to work in the mines and plantations of Southeast Asia, the British West Indies, Spanish Cuba, Australia and California.[5] An official commission was sent to Cuba in 1873-1874 to investigate allegations of ill-treatment and in 1877 a treaty signed between China and Spain provided for the establishment of a Chinese consulate in Havana. A Chinese envoy to the US, Spain and Peru was appointed in 1875, although he did not actually take up his position until 1878; after the creation of a permanent diplomatic mission in Washington Chinese consulates were opened in San Francisco and New York.[6] Meanwhile, a Chinese mission of apology sent to Britain following the death of a British consular official in south China in 1875 was converted into China's first permanent embassy abroad. Guo Songdao (1818-1891) was chosen as head of the mission, which left China in December 1876.[7] As ambassador to Britain Guo arranged for the establishment of a Chinese consulate in Singapore in 1877 and in the following year Guo himself was named as concurrent ambassador to France. Chinese embassies were also opened in Germany (1877), Japan (1878) and Russia (1879).

China's defeat by Japan in 1894-95 (in a war fought over which country would exercise hegemony in Korea), graphically illustrated by the destruction of the Beiyang (Northern) fleet that had been created in 1888, has conventionally been viewed as marking the failure of self-strengthening, after which more radical institutional change was sought to bring about 'wealth and power' (*fuqiang*). General accounts of the period note that self-strengthening was hampered by its uncoordinated nature and lack of long-term planning. Projects were mainly initiated and directed by a few provincial officials; the fact that they could be transferred or dismissed at any time by the court meant that such projects were always potentially vulnerable if incoming officials were not enthusiastic supporters. There was little positive direction from the centre and the court often seemed immobilized as a result of factional rivalries between traditionalists and supporters of self-strengthening. Such factional rivalries were often manipulated by the Empress Dowager Cixi (who assumed regency powers on behalf of her nephew, Emperor Guangxu, following the death of her own son, the Tongzhi Emperor in 1875) as a means of preserving her own power and influence. Other factors mentioned that adversely affected self-strengthening include technical backwardness, corruption, a shortage of capital and the diversion of potential investment funds to meet increasing military expenditures in the wake of foreign threats on China's land and maritime frontiers.[8] Another factor often overlooked was the non-Chinese origins of the dynasty itself, established by Manchu peoples from the north-east in 1644. Anxious to avoid accusations of betraying the Confucian cultural patrimony, Cixi frequently wavered between support for change and defence of the status quo.

THE HISTORIOGRAPHICAL DEBATE

In the 1950s and 60s historians tended to take the failure of self-strengthening for granted and to attribute such a failure to the inadequacies of traditional Confucian thought and practice in adapting to the modern world.[9] Mary Wright's *The Last Stand of Chinese Conservatism*, which focused on the period coinciding with the reign of Emperor Tongzhi (1860-74) and known as the Tongzhi Restoration, argued that the goal of Restoration leaders in the wake of the Taiping Rebellion 'was an austere and stable agrarian society in which a strongly inculcated ideal of frugality curbed the cost of government, the luxuries of the gentry, and the material aspirations of the peasantry'.[10] Since there was no desire to create a new society, Wright claimed, Restoration leaders only had a limited notion of change compared with reformist thought of the 1890s. Thus there was simply no recognition of the need either to expand agricultural production (thereby increasing agrarian-based revenues) or to exploit new and expanded sources of revenue. The priority for leaders such as Li Hongzhang was to restore the health of the traditional economy rather than to enhance the country's wealth at the expense of its traditional institutions.[11] Confucian aversion both to acquisitiveness among the people (including elites) and to state intervention in the economy, combined with traditional official distrust of activities such as mining (because of the potentially disruptive effects it might have on social order), meant that commerce, foreign trade and modern machines were all disparaged.[12] Ultimately, Wright concluded, the Restoration failed 'because the requirements for maintaining the Confucian social order and the requirements for ensuring China's survival in the modern world had proved quite fundamentally opposed'.[13]

As will be discussed later, studies from the 1970s on who would take issue with Wright's rather rigid and stereotyped description of Confucian thought did not allow for an appreciation of the different traditions within Confucianism and how some of those very traditions could be enlisted in the cause of pragmatic reform. Also, while Wright had focused on key provincial and court leaders during the 1860s and early 1870s (implying that no further significant developments took place before the late 1890s), later historians would extend their gaze beyond the early 1870s, arguing that a noticeable evolution of thinking *did* occur before the late 1890s amongst a wider constituency that included reformist scholars and merchant-compradors as well as officials.

Two of the earlier studies that did go beyond the 1870s likewise assumed the failure of self-strengthening and, like Wright, attributed the failure to the negative impact of traditional thought and government practice. A.Feuerwerker, *China's Early Industrialization: Sheng Hsuan-huai and Mandarin Enterprise (1958)* focused on a number of modern enterprises established and overseen by officials but entrusted to merchant management (*guandu shangban*: 'official supervision and merchant management'). These included the China Merchants' Steam Navigation Company (1872), the Kaiping Coal Mines (1877), the Shanghai Cotton Cloth Mill (1878), the Imperial Telegraph Administration (1881) and the Hanyang Ironworks (1896). Feuerwerker argued that these *guandu shangban* enterprises neither ushered in an industrial revolution nor stimulated an institutional breakthrough because they represented a compromise with traditional institutions and patterns of behaviour. In other words, they 'provided a vehicle whereby the overwhelming inertia of an imperial political system and Confucian ideology, the basis of which was a society founded on pre-scientific intensive agriculture, could be adjusted to the compelling need for modern industry and means of communication'.[14] Feuerwerker noted that officials such as Li Hongzhang and Zhang Zhidong founded these modern enterprises not to promote fundamental social change but rather to enhance their own regional power on the one hand, and to hold off further Western encroachment while efforts were made to strengthen the foundations of China's traditional political and social order on the other. Furthermore, nepotism, corruption and particularistic considerations hampered the running of the enterprises themselves.[15] Far from becoming the engines of economic growth they eventually became institutions for the protection of bureaucratic capital. Although Feuerwerker suggested that these enterprises had to cope with other problems such as foreign competition, a weak central government, inadequate capital and technical backwardness, ultimately it was 'deficient motivation' (defined as a 'psycho-ideological block') that played the key role in the obstruction of a solution to these problems and the failure to bring about institutional change that might overcome the 'weight of family and local ties, the low valuation of mercantile and industrial activity, and the shortcomings of the traditional relations between official and merchant'.[16] In the final analysis, Feuerwerker echoed Wright in asserting that the requirements for modernization were incompatible with traditional Confucian thought and practice.[17]

A similar thesis was adopted by a study of China's naval development during the nineteenth century.[18] Although a naval board (*shuishi yamen*) was created in 1885 and regional fleets organized (the most important of which was the Beiyang fleet) with the aim of protecting the Confucian tradition against Western aggression, no professional modern naval force materialized because of the fundamental contradiction 'between the Confucian institutions and the modern naval means which were created to defend them'.[19] The convictions that naval officials possessed were informed by Confucian values, which prevented the development of a well-trained and professional naval service that identified with the interests of the 'state' or 'nation' rather than with particularistic loyalties.[20]

Since the 1970s there has been a shift away from the paradigm that assumed a fundamental incompatibility between Confucianism and modernization.[21] Scholars on the one hand have explored other factors (both endogenous and exogenous) that might have hampered the self-strengthening movement and, on the other, have concerned themselves less with why the movement 'failed' than with analysing longer term changes in reform thought, commercial development and modern state building.

As far as exogenous factors are concerned, scholars in the 1970s began to debate the role of imperialism as a key factor in determining China's political, economic and social development. Some argued that the Western presence in China distorted the economy and prevented the emergence of a strong central government capable of promoting indigenous industrial development. Foreign imports spelled doom for some domestic handicrafts; the lack of tariff autonomy (as a result of the unequal treaties) meant that China could not protect its infant industries or reshape the pattern of its foreign trade; key sectors of the economy (such as mining and railways) became exclusively foreign concerns; foreign enterprises in the treaty ports (protected by extraterritoriality), which were mainly concerned with speculation, banking and foreign trade, attracted Chinese investment capital that might have been used for domestic industrialization; and the Qing government's increasing indebtedness to the foreign powers fatally weakened its freedom of manoeuvre.[22] Ultimately it was not institutional or cultural factors that explained China's failure to modernize but its incorporation into the global capitalist economy.[23] Another study that highlighted the negative impact of imperialism took issue with Feuerwerker, claiming that until the 1890s Chinese-controlled industrialization *was* gaining momentum because of a 'mutually supportive interaction of official aid and enterprise success'.[24] *Guandu shangban* enterprises like the China Merchants' Steam Navigation Company and the Kaiping Mines, supported by Qing officials and financed by Chinese merchant capital, achieved success in competing with foreign interests and displacing foreign imports. It was only after 1897, with more extensive foreign intervention and the government's growing burden of loan and indemnity payments, that most of these enterprises stagnated.

Other studies focusing on endogenous factors have highlighted both the limited nature of bureaucratic reform after 1860 and the failure to counter the influence of local elites to demonstrate that dynastic revival in the post-Taiping period represented only a 'temporary stabilization'.[25] With regard to economic factors, recent explorations of China's tea and silk trades have pointed out that although the late Qing economy *was* flexible and *could* respond successfully to opportunities provided by growing world demand, ultimately such increased trade did not lead to structural transformation.[26] Thus tea cultivation expanded considerably from the eighteenth century onwards; shipments of tea from the port of Fuzhou alone rose from 35 million lbs in 1856–57 to over 96 million lbs in 1880. Until the last two decades of the nineteenth century, in fact, China was the world's largest supplier of tea. The problem was that tea cultivation was dispersed amongst thousands of small-scale producers using manual processing methods and that the growing, processing and distribution of tea remained unintegrated. This meant that by the end of the nineteenth century China's tea trade was increasingly vulnerable to competition from British-owned tea plantations in India, which carried out production on a massive scale using machine technology. Likewise, silk became a leading export commodity in response to growing world demand during the latter half of the nineteenth century.[27] Again, however, Chinese silk ultimately became vulnerable to foreign (Japanese) competition because of the absence of government leadership in ensuring quality control and the stifling effect of internal taxes and export duties.[28]

Another approach that seeks to break from the earlier deterministic assumption that Confucianism and modernization were incompatible has been to highlight a tradition of pragmatic reform thought within Confucianism that predated the Western impact and on which officials and scholars could draw during the latter half of the nineteenth century.[29] For example, in the early years of the nineteenth century scholars associated with the School of Practical Statecraft (*jingshi*) championed administrative reform, insisting that government be judged by its usefulness and practicality. The idea emerged that it was legitimate for the state to strive for profit (*li*), in other words to seek wealth and power. Such a quest would entail granting more economic freedom to merchants, whose services would also be actively sought by officials.[30] Recent studies have also noted how traditionally-derived concepts could acquire new meanings as they were adapted to novel situations. Thus the term *bianfa*, which had referred in the early nineteenth century to minor adjustments to administrative methods, increasingly came to mean 'fundamental reforms' after the 1860s. Another traditional term, *quan* (authority), began to be used in the late 1860s to refer to China's inherent rights as in 'economic rights' (*liquan*), defined by Li Hongzhang as a country's right to exercise autonomy over its own financial affairs.[31] Soon the term would be used in discussions concerning the need to compete with the West for economic benefits and hence 'retrieve lost economic rights' (*shouhui liquan*). Likewise, the term *shangzhan* (lit: 'commercial warfare'), which had originally referred in the early 1860s to the taxing of commerce in order to provide revenues for the suppression of rebellion, was used from the late 1870s on to signify the development of industry and commerce so as to drive out foreign economic interests and compete for markets abroad.[32]

This has led some historians to argue that the period of self-strengthening from the 1860s to 1890s witnessed the emergence of an 'economic (or commercial) nationalism' that anticipated the more widespread nationalism of the early twentieth century when gentry élites, merchants and students denounced the inequities of the unequal treaty system, foreign economic privilege and the treatment of their compatriots abroad.[33] In this sense the Confucian officials involved in the promotion of self-strengthening enterprises are seen more as key transitional figures linking the nineteenth century with the state-building and modernization projects of the twentieth than as the symbols of a doomed Confucian order.[34] An important new study of one such official, Shen Baozhen (1820-1879), reveals that it was quite possible to be both a Confucian and an advocate of radical change.[35] Shen, the governor of Jiangxi province from 1862 to 1867, abandoned an official career in 1867 to become for the next eight years the director of China's first modern naval dockyard at Fuzhou. As such he was the first high-ranking official to take personal charge of a modern defence industry, a decision that was motivated by patriotic concerns rather than personal opportunism.[36]

Shen's sensitivity to the country's loss of its 'economic rights' (*liquan*) and the impairment of its administrative integrity (*shiquan*) also explained his earlier resistance (in 1865) to the introduction of railroads and telegraphs which, he believed, would be a potential tool for increased foreign control. Later, as Governor-general of Liangjiang (Jiangsu, Anhui, Jiangxi) in

1877, he would dismantle the first railway built in China. A ten-mile track running from Shanghai to Woosung, it had been built in 1876 entirely with foreign capital (and with no permission from local authorities). Rather than evidence of diehard conservatism hostile to Western technology, Shen's action was more the reassertion of Chinese sovereignty and an attempt to halt further foreign control of the country's economy.[37]

Shen clearly envisaged a coherent programme of reform; for him the Fuzhou dockyard represented the foundation (and not the limits) of defence modernization. For example, he later proposed that a knowledge of mathematics be tested in the Confucian civil service examinations, sent students from the dockyard's naval school to Europe for advanced technical training, and pioneered modern coal mining (initially to provide convenient sources of fuel for the ships produced at the dockyard). Such a programme of reform, it is argued, suggests that self-strengthening was more dynamic and comprehensive than was hitherto assumed; it therefore should be viewed as the beginnings of modern state building.[38] In the process the patriotism of officials such as Shen Baozhen was transformed into a conscious nationalism, keenly aware that the nation-state's interests overrode all individual and particularistic loyalties.[39]

There has also been a reassessment of Li Hongzhang, perhaps the most influential official during the self-strengthening period.[40] A key figure in the suppression of the Taiping rebellion as the commander of one of the regional militia armies sanctioned by the Qing court, Li served as Governor-general of the metropolitan province of Zhili from 1870 to 1895. During his long tenure he initiated, or became associated with, a wide range of self-strengthening projects that included arms manufacture, shipping, mining and railroads. Often viewed in the past as an opportunistic official who exploited modern enterprises to enhance his regional power (thus also symbolising the Qing dynasty's loss of centralized control in the latter half of the nineteenth century),[41] scholars such as Kwang-ching Liu have noted that Li's policy initiatives and reform proposals were consistently underpinned by a patriotic determination to recover China's 'economic rights' and to prevent further Western encroachment.[42] His setting up of the China Merchants Steam Navigation Company in 1872, for example, was motivated by a desire to compete with foreign steamship lines, which monopolized the coastal trade. Like the early nineteenth century statecraft scholars who had urged official encouragement of merchant enterprise to bring about wealth and strength,[43] Li also emphasized the importance of utilizing merchant capital and managerial talent to run the enterprise. As China's first joint-stock company (*gongsi*) Li protected the enterprise from bureaucratic interference as well as arranging for the provision of cheap government loans and bestowing it with monopoly rights to convey government tax rice from the south to the capital.[44] Li's decision to set up the China Merchants Steam Navigation Company is thus viewed as being influenced by a 'commercial nationalism' aiming to divert the profits of foreign enterprises into the hands of Chinese.[45] Moreover, it is argued, the successful performance of the company, at least until 1885 when increasing bureaucratic control and growing financial pressures led to stagnation, demonstrated that the government *could* play a positive role in the setting up of modern enterprises.[46]

Finally, historians since the 1970s have increasingly recognized the important contributions made by a non-official constituency to self-strengthening and the evolution of reform thought. Referred to as 'coastal reformers'[47] or 'the treaty port community',[48] many of them were missionary-educated, had studied or travelled abroad, or were employed as compradors by foreign firms in the treaty ports.[49] Their cosmopolitan outlook and commitment to Sino-Western commerce, however, did not preclude a keen sense of economic nationalism stressing the dynamic function of commerce and industry in improving the people's livelihood and competing with Western interests. This nationalism also made them pioneering advocates of institutional reform.[50] Members of this treaty port community were employed by officials to manage enterprises like the China Merchants Steam Navigation Company or were attached to the personal staffs of provincial officials. Referred to as *mufu* (lit: 'tent government') this personal staff system drew on a long tradition whereby officials recruited advisers on an unofficial and personal basis. During the latter half of the nineteenth century the system greatly expanded as self-strengthening officials increasingly came to depend on the technical expertise of merchant-compradors and scholars with extensive knowl-edge of the West.[51] Some were used as foreign policy advisers and one scholar has highlighted the key role they played in bringing about a more nationalistic conception of foreign affairs (that included calling for the abolition of extraterritoriality and the return of China's economic sovereignty), anticipating the rights recovery movement of the early twentieth century when gentry elites mobilized capital to buy back foreign railroad and mining concessions. One interesting example of this phenom-enon was merchant cooperation with the government in the attempt to enhance China's economic presence in Korea during the 1880s and 1890s at a time when increasing Japanese encroachment there was threatening China's traditional political influence.[52]

A significant, although often overlooked, member of this group of 'coastal reformers' was Ma Jianzhong, who became one of the most active members of Li Hongzhang's *mufu*.

THE LIFE AND THOUGHT OF MA JIANZHONG

Ma Jianzhong (1845-1900) was born in Dantu prefecture, Jiangsu province and came from a family of Catholics that traced their conversion back to the seventeenth century at a time when Jesuits had been active in China.[53] His father, originally the owner of a herbal shop and part-time practitioner of medicine, later became a rice and silk merchant. One of Ma's elder brothers, Ma Xiangbo (1840-1939), was to become a prominent educator in the last years of the Qing and early years of the Republic.[54] In 1852 Ma enrolled in a French Catholic school in Shanghai (the *Xuhui gongxue*), where he studied Greek, Latin, French, English and mathematics.[55] When the court sanctioned a proposal by Li Hongzhang and Shen

Baozhen in 1876 to send a group of students from the Fuzhou
Naval Dockyard school to Europe for further training, Ma was
appointed as a diplomatic attaché to accompany the mission.
Comprising twenty-six students and three apprentices under the
joint supervision of the Dockyard's French director, Prosper
Giquel, and a Chinese official, Li Fengbao, the mission left in
March 1877.[56] Since the Fuzhou naval school had both English
and French language divisions some of the students attended the
Royal Naval College at Greenwich while others studied ship
construction, metallurgy and mining in France.[57]

During the ensuing three years he was in France Ma used the
opportunity to acquire a broad knowledge of international law.
He attended lectures at the Ecole Libre des Sciences
Politiques[58] in Paris from November 1877 to June 1879,
taking examinations in international law, commercial law and
political systems. At the same time he studied at the Faculty of
Law, earning the distinction of being the first Chinese student
to gain the *baccalauréat* and, in 1879, a *licence de droit* (Law
Diploma). When a Chinese embassy was opened in Paris in
1878 Ma served in the translation section and was awarded
official rank.[59] On his return to China in 1880 Ma became an
active member of Li Hongzhang's personal staff, being sent to
India in 1881 (to discuss ways of ending the opium trade) and
helping to draw up a draft treaty between Korea and the US in
1881-1882.[60]

Traditionally, Korea had been China's tributary and Li
Hongzhang, in virtual charge of China's foreign policy (as
Governor-general of metropolitan Zhili and Imperial Commissioner for the Northern Ports), sought to encourage Korea's
opening to the West as well as to enhance China's own political
and economic influence there as a means to thwart Japan's
perceived ambitions to play a dominant role in the Korean
peninsula. The draft treaty that Ma helped draw up was in fact
agreed upon by Li Hongzhang and the American envoy,
Commodore Shufeldt, before being formally signed by the
Korean king in May 1882.[61] After he had accompanied
Shufeldt to Korea for the formal signing of the US-Korean
Treaty of Friendship and Commerce Ma became involved in

negotiating Sino-Korean trade regulations that gave Chinese merchants considerable advantages over their foreign counterparts. Along with Tang Tingshu, the merchant manager of the China Merchants' Steam Navigation Company, Ma also arranged in October 1882 for a Chinese loan to Korea designed to cement Sino-Korean economic ties. The loan, to be financed by the China Merchants Steam Navigation Company and the Kaiping Coal Mines, was repayable in twelve years with the Korean customs revenue to serve as security. The agreement also allowed for the future exploitation of Korean mineral resources by the Kaiping Coal Mining Company if interest repayments could not be made.[62]

By early 1884 Ma had been appointed assistant manager of the China Merchants Steam Navigation Company, a position he retained until 1891. During the Sino-French War (1884-1885) he supervised the temporary transfer of the company's fleet to the American firm of Russell and Co. in order to avoid its confiscation by the enemy (the fleet was returned to Chinese ownership in 1885). In 1896 Ma accompanied Li Hongzhang to Moscow for the coronation ceremony of Czar Nicholas II. He died in Shanghai at the height of the Boxer uprising. During his last years Ma completed a pioneering work on Chinese grammar, which was published in 1904.[63]

The activities of Ma Jianzhong and Tang Tingshu in Korea have been described in terms of a new economic or mercantile nationalism that pervaded reformist thought in the latter half of the nineteenth century and influenced foreign policy-making officials such as Li Hongzhang.[64] In the case of Korea this entailed an active pursuit of Chinese economic interests as a means of safeguarding China's national prestige and security.[65] Implicit in this new economic nationalism was the novel idea that commerce, far from being a parasitic offshoot of the rural economy (as some orthodox Confucians might have assumed), was vital to national survival and prosperity.[66] Reformist thought from the 1860s on increasingly referred to China as a country having commercial and economic interests as well as cultural ones.[67]

Ma Jianzhong was one of the more intriguing representatives

of this new way of thinking because, unlike many of his contemporaries, he was well versed in Western studies (through his French Catholic education in Shanghai) and he achieved notable scholarly success in Europe. Ma was not the first Chinese scholar to spend an extended time in Europe of course. That distinction belongs to Wang Tao (1828-1897), described by one historian as the forerunner of the 'treaty port intellectual'.[68] Wang served as the Chinese editor for the London Missionary Society's press in Shanghai in 1849 and in 1862 assisted the Scottish missionary, James Legge, with the translation of the Confucian Classics. By this time Wang was advocating the use of Western methods (*xifa*) in mining, shipbuilding and the manufacture of agricultural machinery, as well as suggesting that the Chinese government adopt a more enlightened attitude towards merchants.[69] Wang accompanied Legge when he returned to his native Scotland in 1868 and stayed there for the next two years, during which time he visited England and France. On his return to China Wang embarked on a full time career of journalism and continued to support the adoption of Western technology and government promotion of commerce.[70]

Similar ideas were also championed by both prominent compradors such as Zheng Guanying (1842-1923)[71] and 'hinterland reformers' such as Xue Fucheng (1842-1923).[72] Xue Fucheng, a lower-level degree holder and member of Li Hongzhang's *mufu* who served in a number of official posts before being appointed Chinese Ambassador to Britain and France in 1890, submitted reform proposals in 1879 that have been described as the first comprehensive plan for change.[73] He recommended that commerce and industry be expanded, that the government adopt an active role in the building of modern transportation and communications systems and that Western science be widely studied. Such changes, he argued, were the best means both to adapt to changing international circumstances and protect China's traditional culture (the ancient Way of China's sage kings and philosophers).

A more detailed exposition of such reform ideas, however, can already be found in Ma Jianzhong's writings produced while he was in France (Texts 1-4). Based on his intimate knowledge of Western culture, Ma discussed government sponsorship and protection of commerce, the importance of public trust in the mobilization of capital, the building and financing of railroads, and the role of international law and diplomacy. His writings were characterized by a keen appreciation of Western political systems and society (although this did not preclude criticism) as well as a sensitivity to the way China was perceived and treated by the West. Unlike thinkers such as Wang Tao and Xue Fucheng, Ma did not cite precedents from China's own history to justify reform or argue that change was perfectly compatible with preserving the Way of China's classical past. For Ma change was justified solely on the grounds that it would augment state revenues and improve the people's livelihood. Throughout his writings he used the term *Zhongguo* to refer to China rather than the more traditional *tianxia* (lit: 'all under Heaven'). As one historian has noted, this marked the emergence of a national consciousness in which the traditional sinocentric worldview gave way to the assumption that China was a nation state competing for survival in an international arena with other nation states.[74] Intriguingly, despite Ma's Catholic upbringing and education, he did not comment on the role of Christianity in Western culture. Whereas the later reformer Kang Youwei would frequently refer to the role of Christianity in cultivating a morally upright, disciplined and united citizenry in the West (and on this basis advocating the establishment of Confucianism as a state religion), Ma preferred to emphasize the protection of commerce and the trust that existed between government and people as the sources of Western wealth and strength.

In a letter sent to Li Hongzhang in 1878 recording his examination success at the Ecole Libre des Sciences Politiques (Text 1) Ma provided details of his course of studies.[75] In addition to taking examinations on international diplomacy, political systems and foreign trade, he also wrote examination answers on commercial legislation. Noting that the source of Western prosperity lay with the protection of commerce and the implementation of good laws rather than the use of machinery, Ma concluded that ensuing public confidence and support had facilitated the mobilization of investment funds needed to finance railroads and industry. Other notable features of Western societies, Ma asserted, such as school systems, parliaments, industrial strength and military prowess, all derived from commercial prosperity and mutual trust between government and people.

Ma's conviction that a flourishing commerce, in which both the state and people had a vital stake, was the crucial factor in Western progress meant that he was not always overawed by Western technology as were some Chinese diplomats in Europe.[76] In his letter to Li Hongzhang Ma mentions that he visited the Paris Exhibition while taking a break from his studies, expressing his disappointment that there had been no technological breakthroughs in the military, mining and textile manufacturing spheres. He was not impressed either with the new inventions of the telephone and the phonograph, asserting that they only had novelty value.

On the other hand, Ma was clearly impressed with what he called 'good laws and government' in the West (Text 1). One of the topics on which he wrote for the examinations at the Ecole Libre des Sciences Politiques involved a discussion of the various political constitutions in Western countries. Ma emphasized the benefits of a system in which the legislative, executive and judicial powers were separated. According to Ma, this prevented abuse of the law by corrupt officials and arbitrary interference in people's lives. Significantly, Ma also highlighted the fact that everyone in society would therefore enjoy autonomy and a feeling of self-respect, further cementing the trust between government and people. In another letter sent from Paris (Text 2) Ma elaborated further on the characteristic features of Western societies, which he listed as including individual prosperity, free expression of public opinion through parliament, efficient and corruption-free taxation systems, fair and just legal procedures, public cleanliness and safety, and the ability of people to live and work without interference from others. Ma's positive assessment of Western society was similar to that of Guo Songdao, China's first Ambassador to Britain and

France (1877-1879) who is often considered one of the first Chinese scholars to write positively about Western political institutions and cultural values (rather than simply advocating the adoption of Western technology). It is true that in his journal Guo asserted that Western culture was founded on firm principles of justice, honour, order and discipline,[77] but Ma's emphasis on individual autonomy was unprecedented. Also, in contrast to the later reform writings of Yan Fu (1854-1921), the translator of Adam Smith, John Stuart Mill and Charles Darwin who perceived a utilitarian link between the encouragement of individual interests in the West and the emergence of powerful and wealthy states,[78] Ma seemed to praise individual autonomy for its own sake.

At the same time, however, Ma perceptively noted the gap between appearance and reality in Western political systems (Text 1). Referring to Britain Ma pointed out that although parliament seemed to be at the centre of government in practice real power was exercised by the prime minister and his cabinet colleagues.[79] Ma also argued that in the US the presidential elections were tainted by widespread corruption and the spoils system, whereby members of the incoming president's clique were awarded government posts. Such blatant nepotism, Ma lamented, belied the image of a public-minded president devoted to the general good.

Another theme of Ma's writings from France was the need for China to train a professional diplomatic service, perhaps the first proposal of its kind in Chinese reformist thought.[80] In another letter written in 1878 (Text 2) Ma recommended that China, having been persuaded by the Western powers to establish diplomatic missions abroad,[81] should turn the situation to its own advantage. Although Ma thought that Western countries themselves welcomed the creation of Chinese embassies more out of a feeling of self importance than an altruistic desire to improve international understanding, he insisted that this should not inhibit China from training professional, knowledgeable and socially adept diplomats who could advance China's interests in the world as well as providing accurate and significant information on the countries in which they were posted. Most diplomatic posts at the present time, Ma complained, were merely sinecures held by opportunistic incompetents lacking linguistic and social skills. He proposed the establishment of a diplomats' college in Shanghai that would provide training in foreign languages, history and science. After a probationary year working abroad, trainees would then study international law and diplomacy for a further two years at another college to be set up within the Chinese embassy in Paris. Ma suggested that these new training colleges would be financed by eliminating all sinecure posts in Chinese embassies. Ma concluded with the radical suggestion that the professional diplomats of the future might be able to play an important role in government, traditionally the monopoly of the classically-trained Confucian scholar.

Underpinning Ma's proposal for a professional diplomatic service was a sensitivity to China's image in the West, a feature of much reformist thought at the end of the nineteenth century.[82] He was at pains to point out that the lack of social skills demonstrated by Chinese diplomats was a source of ridicule in their host countries and hence contributed to a lowering of China's prestige. This concern was also evident in Ma's letter to Li Hongzhang (Text 1), in which he criticized the lacklustre Chinese display at the Paris Exhibition. The poor and amateurish quality of the objects displayed, Ma lamented, not only put China in a bad light but also meant that the display could not even rival that exhibited by Japan! This implicit condescension towards Japan, shared by many Chinese officials and scholars in the late nineteenth and early twentieth centuries, was itself quite ironic since Ma himself was painfully aware of Western condescension towards the Chinese. Noting that the high marks he received in the examinations were praised by the examiners and the Parisian press (Text 1), Ma wrote that it was the very fulsomeness of the praise that unnerved him. For Ma such exalted praise was really an expression of surprise that a Chinese could demonstrate scholarly intelligence.

Ma's third main preoccupation in his writings of this period concerned the building and financing of railroads in China. During the late 1870s and 1880s there was a vigorous debate over the merits and disadvantages of railroads. As noted earlier, the first railway built in China (the Shanghai-Woosung line completed in 1877) had been dismantled by Governor-general Shen Baozhen because of fears that it would increase foreign control of China's economy.[83] The predominant official attitude towards railroads has been described as one of indifference; trains were perceived as mere 'toys' rather than the means to enhance economic development.[84] Some officials warned that railroads would cause popular unrest because they might disturb graves and violate principles of geomancy (*fengshui*).[85] Liu Xihong, who was Guo Songdao's assistant at the Chinese Embassy in London, doubted whether railroads would ever be profitable because the people were too poor to purchase train tickets and the volume of freight moved would be too small; furthermore, the railroads would be saddled with a heavy debt burden. In the late 1880s another official, Yu Lianyun, objected to the idea of building a line from Tianjin to Tongzhou (the terminus for canal shipments to Beijing) on the grounds that it would throw millions of people out of a job and hence aggravate social unrest.[86]

Nevertheless, Li Hongzhang managed to gain approval in 1880 for the construction of a six mile mule-drawn tramway to transport coal from the Kaiping mines (at Tangshan) to a nearby canal at Xukezhuang, which was completed in 1881. Shortly afterwards a steam locomotive began operations on the line, which was later extended to Lutai in 1886 and then Tianjin in 1888.[87] However, a proposal to build a line from Tangshan to Tongzhou (thirteen miles east of the capital) was rejected in 1888 because of the proximity of imperial tombs.[88] Railroad construction had therefore been a slow and hesitant process; by 1897 there were just 270 miles of railway track under Chinese control.

Ma Jianzhong's two essays on railroads written in 1879 were perhaps the first detailed proposals confidently proclaiming the benefits of railroad construction. In the first of the two essays (Text 3) Ma argued that railroads would help alleviate natural disasters, encourage the exploitation of natural resources, facilitate migration from overpopulated regions to less populated ones, discourage criminal activity by bandits and corrupt local officials (because speedier communications would keep central government officials abreast of local situations), provide cheaper food (by preventing grain price fluctuations) and stimulate increased trade. In the process, Ma insisted, both the people's livelihood and state revenues would be enhanced.[89] Ma also suggested that railroads would protect China's strategic interests. Whereas critics warned that railroads would provide the opportunity for foreigners to impose military and economic control in China (often citing India as a precedent), Ma preferred to stress the growing threat to China's frontiers posed by railroads already being built by Russia (in central Asia), Britain (in India, Nepal and Burma) and France (in Vietnam). These countries, Ma asserted would soon be in a position to encroach on China's frontier regions and hence threaten the fragmentation of the country. Railroads would enable the government to transfer troops quickly and efficiently to any potential trouble-spot on the frontiers. It is significant to note that many of Ma's arguments in favour of railroads were repeated almost *ad verbatim* by Zhang Zhidong, the Governor-general of Hunan and Hubei, when he memorialized the throne in 1889 proposing the construction of a line from Hankou to Beijing.[90]

Ma's essay also provided details on the construction and management of railroads. Referring to developments in the West, he suggested that government-owned railroads would be unsuitable because they would be used solely for military purposes, whereas merchant-owned companies would be unfeasable because cutthroat market competition would lead to bankruptcy. He preferred a system of merchant-government cooperation whereby government would lease land to merchant-managed companies as well as providing subsidies and acting as a loan guarantor. A number of enterprises, organized under the rubric *guanshang heban* (official-merchant cooperation), were in fact set up in the 1880s and 1890s.[91]

Ma also discussed the organization of train travel, describing how passenger traffic was divided into first, second and third class categories,[92] and explained the complexities of fare regulations, noting, for example, that children should be charged half-price. In his description of the management structure of train stations Ma particularly emphasized efficient personnel supervision and the centralization of budgetary procedures. Interestingly, he also referred to the practice of awarding staff retirement pensions.

In the second of his two essays on railroads (Text 4) Ma recommended that a foreign loan be used. Referring to the concept of a national debt, Ma pointed out that all governments had borrowed funds to finance industrialization. Such funds had been forthcoming, he claimed, because the public had confidence in government credibility and the future profit-ability of enterprises. Unfortunately, Ma noted, the government in China could not resort to public borrowing because of people's straitened economic circumstances; there was no alternative to seeking foreign loans. Ma suggested, however, that the treaty port banks be bypassed and that such loans be sought directly in Western countries; ideally money would be borrowed to purchase rolling stock directly from the manufacturers. He was careful to distinguish between lending and investment, rejecting the idea of foreign share ownership in China's future railways. Furthermore, in answer to potential criticism that China would be burdened by debt, Ma confidently predicted that the huge profits gained from the railroads would quickly pay off the loans. Ma broke new ground when he advocated the use of foreign loans (negotiated directly in the West) to stimulate future economic development. Before 1894, for example, the nine foreign loans that *had* been contracted (totalling 40 million taels) were principally for defence and other immediate needs and had been obtained through foreign firms in the treaty ports.[93]

Ma concluded his essay with a proposal to build a line from Tianjin to Beijing, again a radical idea for its time given the sensitivity felt by traditionalists to the prospect of a railway approaching the capital. Ma maintained that such a line would serve as the model for a future national network. It would arouse popular enthusiasm because of increased trade and new employment opportunities, as well as providing a valuable training ground for a future corps of Chinese engineers and managers (and thus avoid the risk of having to depend on foreign experts). Finally the line would demonstrate the virtues of a merchant-run enterprise free from official interference and embezzlement, thereby encouraging future investment.

Ma Jianzhong's most celebrated essay was written in 1890 (Text 5). Significantly entitled 'On Enriching the People' (*Fumin shuo*),[94] it championed the vigorous pursuit of foreign trade and widespread exploitation of natural resources in order to improve the people's standard of living and augment state revenues.[95] Only when commerce and industry flourished and the people prospered, Ma insisted, could the state enjoy wealth and strength. Ma prescribed three measures that had to be undertaken: improvement in the quality of export products, establishment of manufacturing industry, and an active exploitation of natural resources using modern technology.

Although a flourishing export trade was essential to national prosperity, Ma noted, China was experiencing a growing trade imbalance with the West.[96] He particularly lamented the fact that the Chinese tea and silk trades were losing out to Indian and Japanese competition because of inferior quality and high costs. Export figures bore out Ma's concern. Tea exports initially experienced a dramatic boom after the 1830s. Thus exports increased from 81 million lbs (605,000 piculs) in 1840 to 283,157,000 lbs in 1885.[97] By 1890 exports had declined to 222,002,000 lbs; at the same time tea exports from India continued to grow, from 2,707,000 lbs in 1860 to 100,685,000 lbs in 1890.[98] Tea from British-owned plantations in India gradually captured the British market, previously dominated by Chinese teas. In 1896 Britain imported 122,900,000 lbs of tea from India and only 19,800,000 lbs from China.[99] Japanese tea also gradually replaced Chinese tea in the US market. In the late 1860s China had 77% and Japan 19% of the US tea trade in value terms. By the late 1880s and early 1890s the figures were 50% and 43% respectively. On the eve of WW1 Japan had 45% of the US market, whereas China had 18%.[100]

Silk exports, too, enjoyed a dramatic boom. During the 1830s silk exports totalled nearly 10,000 piculs.[101] By 1870 raw silk exports totalled 49,000 piculs.[102] From 1870 to the 1890s exports of raw silk tripled in volume from 49,000 piculs to over 100,000 piculs in the 1890s.[103] In the process raw silk replaced tea as China's major export (in 1887), and was to remain a leading export commodity until the 1930s. Yet, as Ma himself perceptively pointed out, Japanese exports were also consistently expanding at China's expense. Thus whereas in 1890 the total of China's silk exports (80,000 piculs of raw silk and 11,000 piculs of silk fabric) was not much different from that of 1880 (82,000 piculs of raw silk and 8,000 piculs of silk fabric), exports of Japanese raw silk consistently increased from 7,000 piculs in 1870, 15,000 piculs in 1880, and then to 21,000 piculs in 1890. In 1909, just nineteen years after Ma had written his essay, Japan overtook China as the world's leading silk exporter.[104]

Interestingly, while Ma referred to the more efficient and meticulous cultivation methods practised in India and Japan, which meant that their silk and tea was of a more uniform quality, he did not specifically discuss the tea plantation system in India. Rather than focus on the nature of tea production itself in China(which was dispersed amongst thousands of smallholders, who seldom practised monoculture since tea was often intercropped with other cash or subsistence crops),[105] Ma preferred to highlight the weak bargaining position of individual merchants involved in the trade. He asserted that they were vulnerable to price increases from producers and a prey to the deviousness of foreign buyers in the treaty ports. Since tea destined for export was held to be in Chinese possession until paid for by foreign merchants, Chinese dealers were at a disadvantage because they needed a quick cash settlement to cover loan and tax payments.[106] Ma pointed out that foreign buyers deliberately put off payment to increase pressure on Chinese sellers to drive prices down further.[107] The solution, according to Ma, was for merchants to form large joint-stock companies (*gongsi*). With sufficient capital such companies would then be able to buy tea in bulk and would not have to sell quickly to foreign firms at knockdown prices.

In addition to improving the quality of export products and

the formation of merchant joint stock companies, Ma recommended that all inland commercial taxes and export duties be reduced. The principal inland duty was the *lijin*, a surcharge of 1% on the value of commercial goods. Originating as an experiment by a local magistrate in 1853 to raise funds for militia defence against the Taiping rebels, the tax was in force throughout China by 1857.[108] A network of *lijin* tax bureaux was created along waterways and the entrances to major cities, and the tax was either levied on goods in shops and warehouses or collected as a transit tax at various points along trade routes. In Zhejiang and Jiangsu (major silk producing regions) additional silk *lijin* depots were established to tax silk shipments. Tea was also hard hit by taxes. Before 1853 tea taxation had been slight (18-29 cash per picul of packaged tea). In that year a transit tax was levied on tea (*chashui*) in Fujian province. A tea *lijin* tax was added in 1859 and another tea surtax between 1861-1865. This meant that a tax of 0.1485 taels per picul in 1853 increased dramatically to 2.3485 taels per picul.[109]

While the *lijin*, in the words of one scholar, represented an unprecedented intrusion by the state into local marketing systems as a way of gaining additional revenue to meet internal and external crises, reformers such as Ma Jianzhong regarded the *lijin* as an unnecessary hindrance at a time when China (through its exports) needed to compete commercially with the West.[110] Likewise Ma argued that while a reduction in export duties might mean a slight reduction in revenue during the short term, in the long term the inevitable increase in exports would generate more revenue. He also looked forward to the time of treaty revision when tariff rates could be readjusted.[111] Only by means of a vigorous policy of promoting exports, Ma insisted, could China regain its economic rights.

The other two measures Ma recommended were the establishment of manufacturing industry to produce foreign-style goods and hence displace foreign imports, and a more extensive exploitation of China's natural resources (particularly gold and coal). He criticized the poor record of the Shanghai Cotton Cloth Mill, the establishment of which had first been proposed by his patron, Li Hongzhang, in 1878. Officially inaugurated in 1882 it was granted a ten year monopoly to manufacture cotton cloth and yarn. By the time Ma wrote his essay, however, it had barely begun production. He proposed that the mill should receive more investment funds; failing that, he thought more modern textile mills should be built so as to drive out imports of foreign cotton. As in his earlier essay on railroad finance (Text 4), Ma again suggested using a foreign loan to stimulate commerce, industry and the exploitation of natural resources (Ma painted a picture of China as a land of unlimited mineral wealth that demanded to be exploited). Such a loan would be negotiated by a newly created Bureau of Commercial Affairs on behalf of merchant joint-stock companies.

Ma Jianzhong's writings played a crucial role in the circulation of reform ideas in the late nineteenth century, and influenced important provincial officials like Li Hongzhang and Zhang Zhidong. He was a key member of a reform constituency that introduced the concept of economic nationalism and stressed the dynamic role of commerce and foreign trade in bringing about national wealth and strength.[112] Contrary to the assessment of the Self-Strengthening movement made by earlier studies, there was indeed a significant evolution of reform thought in this period. Furthermore, as an active participant in diplomacy and enterprise management, Ma was in a position to put some of his ideas into practice. It is simply not true, as some historians have remarked, that reformers like Ma were powerless individuals without influence.[113] Ma may also have influenced later reformers. The preface to Ma's published works, which appeared in 1896, was written by Liang Qichao (1873-1929), a participant in the 1898 reform movement and later one of the most influential political thinkers during the last decade of the dynasty. Liang recorded having met Ma in Shanghai during the summer of 1896 and expressed his admiration for Ma's breadth of knowledge, especially concerning Western affairs.[114] It is intriguing to note that in 1903 Liang urged the formation of large trusts under government supervision so that China could compete on the world stage,[115] an idea that Ma had first raised in his 1890 essay.

Some of the measures Ma had recommended in that essay were later implemented. Thus in 1898 Fujian province reduced its total inland duty on tea by 19%, while in 1902 the Board of Revenue in Beijing halved the export duty on tea.[116] Also, Ma's urgent call to improve the quality of Chinese silk found an echo in reform proposals of 1898 that advocated the establishment of a national institute of sericulture and the free distribution of disease-free silkworm eggs.[117] Moreover, there was much more active government support for commerce after 1900, something Ma had consistently championed since the late 1870s. A Ministry of Commerce (*Shangbu*) was established in 1903, which later became the Ministry of Agriculture, Industry and Commerce (*Nonggongshangbu*) in 1906. The Ministry sanctioned the creation of merchant chambers of commerce; by 1908 there were 58 General Chambers of Commerce and 223 branch chambers, many of which sponsored and financed commercial and technical schools.[118] Government awards were offered to encourage capital investment in modern enterprises, while tax exemptions were granted to merchants displaying their goods at international fairs. The last years of the dynasty also witnessed the introduction of commercial law. A Commercial Law Office was set up in 1903, which subsequently promulgated laws on company registration (1905) and bankruptcy (1906).[119] Finally, the vigorous demand that Ma and others made in the 1870s and 1880s for China to regain its economic rights was to be echoed in the anti-imperialist movements of the twentieth century.

NOTES

1 These rebellions included that of the Taipings (1851-1864), the Nian (1851-1868), the Miao in Guizhou (1854-1873) and Muslim uprisings in Yunnan (1855-1873) and the north-west (1862-1873).

2 In its general usage, Self-Strengthening refers to the period from the early 1860s to China's defeat at the hands of Japan in 1895. Some historians distinguish the immediate post-Taiping period from the 1880s and 1890s, referring to it as the Restoration (coinciding with the reign of the Emperor Tongzhi 1860-1874) when priority was placed on reviving Confucian ideals of government. See Kwang-ching Liu, 'The Ch'ing Restoration', in D.Twitchett and J.Fairbank (eds), *The Cambridge History of China: vol.10* (Cambridge, 1978),pp.409-490; and Ting-yee Kuo and Kwang-ching Liu, 'Self-Strengthening: The Pursuit of Western Technology', in *ibid.*, pp.491-542. The phrase 'self-strengthening' began to appear from 1861 onwards.

3 For a general discussion of the nature of foreign privilege in China, see A.Feuerwerker, 'The Foreign Presence in China', in J.Fairbank (ed), *The Cambridge History of China: vol.12* (Cambridge, 1983), pp.128-207.

4 For useful chronologies of the Self-Strengthening movement, see K.H.Kim, *Japanese Perspectives on China's Early Modernization: The Self-Strengthening Movement 1860-1895* (Ann Arbor, 1974), pp.3-12; and I.Hsu, *The Rise of Modern China* (New York, 4th ed., 1990), pp.282-287. Hsu rather rigidly divides the period 1861-1895 into three stages: 1861-1872, when the focus was on Western military technology, scientific knowledge and the training of technical and diplomatic personnel with the aim of learning the West's superior techniques in order to control foreigners in China; 1872-1884, when more attention was paid to the development of 'profit-oriented enterprises' such as shipping, railways and mining; and 1885-1895, when the idea of enriching the country through light industry began to gain favour.

5 Yen Ching-hwang, *Coolies and Mandarins: China's Protection of Overseas Chinese During the Late Ch'ing Period 1851-1911* (Singapore, 1985).

6 Shih-san Henry Tsai, *China and the Overseas Chinese in the US 1868-1911* (Fayetteville, 1983); M.Hunt, *The Making of a Special Relationship: The US and China to 1914* (New York, 1983).

7 Excerpts from the journal of Guo Songdao, as well as from those of two of his assistants, Liu Xihong and Zhang Deyi, have been translated in J.Frodsham, *The First Chinese Embassy to the West* (Oxford, 1974). Liu became China's first minister to Germany in 1877, while Zhang Deyi was to become minister to Britain in 1901-1905.

8 See F.Wakeman, *The Fall of Imperial China* (New York, 1975), pp.163-198; I.Hsu, *The Rise of Modern China*, pp.261-294; and J.Spence, *The Search for Modern China* (New York, 1990), pp.194-224. The foreign threats included the Japanese invasion of Formosa (Taiwan) in 1874; the Russian occupation of Ili in Xinjiang in 1871-1881; and the gradual French encroachment and occupation of Vietnam from the 1860s to the 1880s.

9 For a concise introduction to the historiography of the Self-Strengthening movement, see D.Pong, *Shen Pao-chen and China's Modernization in the Nineteenth Century* (Cambridge, 1994), pp.2-23.

10 M.Wright, *The Last Stand of Chinese Conservatism: The T'ung-chih Restoration 1862-1874* (Stanford, 1957), pp.148-149.

11 *ibid.*, pp.63, 148, 149, 153.

12 *ibid.*, pp.150-156.

13 *ibid.*, p.301.

14 A.Feuerwerker, *China's Early Industrialization: Sheng Hsuan-huai and Mandarin Enterprise*

(Cambridge, Mass., 1958), p.242.

15 *ibid.*, pp.242-245. Like Wright, Feuerwerker also noted that official discourse lacked the recognition of the need to increase economic production and revenues.

16 *ibid.*, pp.245-249.

17 Such a dichotomy drew on contemporary Chinese terms referring to the learning and practical application (*yong*) of Western technology as a means of preserving the foundations or essence (*ti*) of China's Confucian tradition.

18 J.Rawlinson, *China's Struggle for Naval Development 1839-1895* (Cambridge, Mass., 1967).

19 *ibid.*, p.201.

20 ibid., p.202. Rawlinson also makes the point, however, that dynastic decline after 1860 may have encouraged naval innovation as much as hindered it. Provincial officials had greater freedom to build dockyards and purchase ships. On the other hand such freedom also increased the opportunities for competition amongst provincial leaders. *ibid.*, pp.199-200.

21 In recent times the paradigm has in fact been stood on its head. The phenomenal economic growth rates of contemporary Singapore, South Korea, Taiwan and south China (all of which belong to the Confucian 'cultural zone') have led analysts to highlight the ways in which Confucian values (e.g. the prestige attributed to education) were successfully adapted to the needs of modernization. For a recent collection of essays that explore the spread and adaptation of Confucian values, see G.Rozman (ed), *The East Asian Region: Confucian Heritage and its Modern Adaptation* (Princeton,1991).

22 See, for example, J.Esherick, 'Harvard on China: The Apologetics of Imperialism', *Bulletin of Concerned Asian Scholars* 4:4 (1972), pp.9-15. Esherick was taking issue with earlier views assuming that foreign investment had made a positive contribution to China's modernization. For an example of such a view, see Hou Chi-ming, *Foreign Investment and Economic Development in China 1840-1937* (Cambridge, Mass., 1965).

23 F.Moulder, *Japan, China and the Modern World Economy: Toward a Reinterpretation of East Asian Development ca.1600 to ca.1918* (Cambridge, 1977). Other studies, however, have argued that the Western economic impact on China was minimal because of the continuing vitality of the traditional economy. See R.Murphey, *The Outsiders: The Western Experience in India and China* (Ann Arbor, 1977). A recent contribution to the debate is T.Wright, 'Imperialism and the Chinese Economy: A Methodological Critique of the Debate', *Bulletin of Concerned Asian Scholars* 18:1 (1986), pp.36-45. Wright argues that those who emphasize the negative economic impact of the Western presence neither take into account its complexity nor consider carefully counter-factual arguments. For an excellent overview of the debate, see P.Cohen, *Discovering History in China* (New York, 1984), chapter 3.

24 S.Thomas, *Foreign Intervention and China's Industrial Development 1870-1911* (Boulder, 1984), p.82.

25 J.Ocko, *Bureaucratic Reform in Provincial China: Ting Jih-ch'ang in Restoration Kiangsu 1867-1870* (Cambridge, Mass., 1983), p.171. Ocko argues that it was the very military success involved in suppressing the Taiping rebellion that vitiated the impetus to reform (*ibid.*, pp.171-172). A similar argument is made by R.Smith, 'Li Hung-chang's Use of Foreign Military Talent: The Formative Period, 1862-1874', in S.Chu and Kwang-ching Liu (eds), *Li Hung-chang and China's Early Modernization* (New York, 1994), pp.119-142. Smith argues that the success of temporary military measures used to suppress the Taipings such as the hiring of foreign mercenaries and the use of Western-style arms stifled the reform impulse.

26 On the tea trade, see R.Gardella, 'Qing Administration of the Tea Trade: Four Facets Over Four Centuries', in J.Leonard and J.Watt (eds), *To Achieve Security and Wealth: The Qing Imperial State and the Economy,1644-1911* (Ithaca, 1992), pp.97-118; and R.Gardella,

Harvesting Mountains: Fujian and the China Tea Trade 1757-1937 (Berkeley, 1994). On the silk trade, see L.Li, *China's Silk Trade: Traditional Industry in the Modern World 1842-1937* (Cambridge, Mass., 1981); and R.Eng, *Economic Imperialism in China: Silk Production and Exports 1861-1932* (Berkeley, 1986).

27 The first Chinese-owned steam filature for silk reeling opened in 1872.

28 The two studies noted above (fn 26), however, have different emphases. Thus while R.Eng notes the lack of government leadership in promoting sericultural reform and the negative impact of internal taxes, he argues that the main problem faced by the silk trade was the weak position in which Chinese silk exporters found themselves vis-a-vis foreign export firms in the treaty ports, since it was these firms that virtually decided on the price and when to pay it. Thus although Western capital played a minimal role in the actual development of silk reeling, Western export firms encouraged speculation through their price manipulations. Such speculation inhibited improvement of quality. L.Li, on the other hand, places the blame squarely on the failure of indigenous commercial practices and institutional arrangements of the silk business. Echoing M.Wright, she maintains that official promotion of sericulture was aimed merely at enhancing local wealth and making the individual household self-sufficient. By the end of the dynasty, she continues, 'neither the concept of a national economic good, nor that of using foreign trade to the nation's advantage had gained much acceptance'. (*China's Silk Trade*, p.138). Like Gardella, she concludes that an opportunity to effect structural and institutional change was missed.

29 A pioneering collection of essays that explored this theme is P.Cohen and J.Schrecker (eds), *Reform in Nineteenth Century China* (Cambridge, Mass., 1976).

30 D.Pong, *Shen Pao-chen and China's Modernization in the Nineteenth Century*, p.16. It should be noted that such reform traditions were highly eclectic, often drawing on ideas from the non-Confucian tradition. One notable statecraft scholar of the early nineteenth century was Wei Yuan, who advocated administrative reform and the reassertion of Chinese naval influence in Southeast Asia as a means of halting the growing Western presence there. See J. Kate Leonard, *Wei Yuan and China's Rediscovery of the Maritime World* (Cambridge, Mass., 1984).

31 D.Pong, 'The Vocabulary of Change: Reformist Ideas of the 1860s and 1870s', in D.Pong and E.Fung (eds), *Ideal and Reality: Social and Political Change in Modern China 1860-1949* (Lanham, 1985), pp.34-35.

32 *ibid.*, p.43.

33 On the emergence of nationalism in the early years of the twentieth century, see A.Iriye, 'Public Opinion and Foreign Policy', in A.Feuerwerker et.al. (eds), *Approaches to Modern Chinese History* (Berkeley, 1967); M.Wright, 'Introduction: The Rising Tide of Change', in M.Wright (ed), *China in Revolution: The First Phase 1900-1913* (New Haven, 1968); and L.Sigel, 'The Treaty Port Commercial Community and the Diplomacy of Chinese Nationalism 1900-1911', in D.Pong and E.Fung (eds), *Ideal and Reality: Social and Political Change in Modern China 1860-1949* (Lanham, 1985).

34 There has also been an interesting shift in mainland Chinese historiography. From the 1950s to 1970s self-strengtheners such as Zeng Guofan and Li Hongzhang were regarded as Chinese traitors, serving the alien Manchu dynasty and collaborating with foreign imperialism. Since the 1980s they have been viewed more as pioneering champions of industrialization.

35 D.Pong, *Shen Pao-chen and China's Modernization in the Nineteenth Century* (Cambridge, 1994).

36 *ibid.*, p.106. Pong also rejects the idea that Shen accepted the appointment out of a desire to enhance his regional power (noting that he was, in fact, an imperial appointee) or because of personal ties with Zuo Zongtang, the Governor-general who had proposed the project in 1866.

37 S.Sturdevant, 'Imperialism, Sovereignty, and Self-Strengthening: A Reassessment of the 1870s', in P.Cohen and J.Schrecker (eds), *Reform in Nineteenth Century China*, pp.63-70.

38 D.Pong, *Shen Pao-chen*, pp.319-321. Shen also advocated reform of the government's budgetary system. It was the ad hoc and uncoordinated nature of the system that always placed self-strengthening enterprises like the Fuzhou dockyard in such a vulnerable financial position.

39 *ibid.*, pp.300-301.

40 See, for example, the collection of essays in S.Chu and Kwang-ching Liu (eds), *Li Hung-chang and China's Early Modernization* (New York, 1994).

41 For an example of such a view, see S.Spector, *Li Hung-chang and the Huai Army: A Study in Nineteenth-Century Chinese Regionalism* (Seattle, 1964).

42 Kwang-ching Liu, 'The Confucian as Patriot and Pragmatist: Li Hung-chang's Formative Years 1823-1866', and Kwang-ching Liu, 'Li Hung-chang in Chihli: The Emergence of a Policy 1870-1875', both in S.Chu and Kwang-ching Liu (eds), *Li Hung-chang and China's Early Modernization*, pp.17-48,49-75. Such concerns prompted Li in the 1860s to look beyond the manufacture of Western weapons. In his 1865 memorial proposing the establishment of the Jiangnan Arsenal Li looked forward to the time when the arsenal might produce machinery that could be used in agriculture and industry. By the early 1870s he was championing the use of Western technology in transport, mining and manufacturing. Liu also points out that Li was as much a metropolitan as a provincial official, particularly as he was concurrently Imperial Commissioner for the Northern Ports. In such a capacity he was frequently consulted by the court over foreign policy and was thus intimately involved with national issues. There was therefore more coordination between the centre and the provinces than hitherto supposed.

43 Kwang-ching Liu, 'The Beginnings of China's Modernization', in S.Chu and Kwang-ching Liu (eds), *Li Hung-chang and China's Early Modernization*, pp.3-5.

44 Such arrangements drew on well established patterns of official cooperation with private merchant groups. See A.McElderry, 'Guarantors and Guarantees in Qing Government-Business Relations', in J.Leonard and J.Watt (eds), *To Achieve Security and Wealth*, pp.119-137.

45 Chi-kong Lai, 'The Qing State and Merchant Enterprise: The China Merchants' Company 1872-1902', in J.Leonard and J.Watt (eds), *To Achieve Security and Wealth*, p.142; Chi-kong Lai, 'Li Hung-chang and Modern Enterprise: The China Merchants' Company 1872-1885', in S.Chu and Kwang-ching Liu (eds), *Li Hung-chang and China's Early Modernization*, p.221.

46 Chi-kong Lai, 'The Qing State and Merchant Enterprise: The China Merchants' Company 1872-1901', pp.142,151. Under the management of two former comprador-merchants, Tang Tingshu and Xu Run, paid-up merchant share capital increased from 180,000 taels to 476,000 taels during 1873. The Company also increased the number of its ships from six in 1874 to 26 in 1880. M.Wright (*The Last Stand of Chinese Conservatism*, pp.176-177), in contrast, thinks that the history of the China Merchants' Steam Navigation Company after 1872 was 'a dismal one'.

47 P.Cohen, 'The New Coastal Reformers', in P.Cohen and J.Schrecker (eds), *Reform in Nineteenth Century China*, pp.255-271; P.Cohen, *Between Tradition and Modernity: Wang T'ao and Reform in Late Ch'ing China* (Cambridge, Mass., 1974), pp.244-245.

48 L.Sigel, 'Foreign Policy Interests and Activities of the Treaty-Port Chinese Community', in P.Cohen and J.Schrecker (eds), *Reform in Nineteenth Century China*, pp.272-281; L.Sigel, 'The Treaty Port Commercial Community and the Diplomacy of Chinese Nationalism 1900-1911', in D.Pong and E.Fung (eds), *Ideal and Reality: Social and Political Change in Modern China 1860-1949*, pp.221-249; L.Sigel, 'Business-Government Cooperation in Late Qing Foreign Policy', in J.Leonard and J.Watt (eds), *To Achieve Security and Wealth*, pp.157-181.

49 On the role of compradors in the economy, see Hao Yen-p'ing, *The Comprador in Nineteenth Century China* (Cambridge, Mass., 1970).

50 For a discussion of reform ideas before the 1890s, see L.Eastman, 'Political Reformism in China Before the Sino-Japanese War', *Journal of Asian Studies*, 27: 4 (August 1968), pp.695-710. P.Cohen ('The New Coastal Reformers', p.259) offers a psychological explanation for the nationalism espoused by the coastal reformers– it was a kind of compensation for the guilt or shame they might have felt by collaborating with Westerners.

51 On the *mufu* system, see K.Folsom, *Friends, Guests and Colleagues: The Mufu System in the Late Ch'ing Period* (Berkeley, 1968). The composition of Li's *mufu* varied over time and totalled hundreds of people.

52 L.Sigel, 'Business-Government Cooperation in Late Qing Korean Policy', in J.Leonard and J.Watt (eds), *To Achieve Security and Wealth: The Qing Imperial State and the Economy, 1644-1911*, pp.157-181.

53 Details on Ma's life and career can be gleaned from the following sources: Banno Masataka, *Chūgoku kindaika to Ba Kenchū* (Ma Jianzhong and China's Modernization), Tokyo, 1985; Chen Sanjing, 'Luelun Ma Jianzhong de waijiao sixiang' (A general discussion of Ma Jianzhong's diplomatic thought), in Zhou Yangshan et.al. (eds), *Jindai Zhongguo sixiang renwu lun: wan Qing sixiang* (Taibei, 1980), pp.470-474; Fang Hao, 'Ma Jianzhong xiansheng shilue' (A biographical sketch of Ma Jianzhong), in Fang Hao, *Fang Hao liushi ziding gao* (Taibei, 1969),vol.2, pp.2026-2028; P.Cohen, *Between Tradition and Modernity: Wang T'ao and Reform in Late Ch'ing China*, pp.250-251; A.Feuerwerker, *China's Early Industrialization: Sheng Hsuan-huai and Mandarin Enterprise*, pp.117-118; K.Folsom, *Friends, Guests and Colleagues: The Mufu System in the Late Ch'ing Period*, pp.139-140; P.Cohen, 'Littoral and Hinterland in Nineteenth Century China: The "Christian Reformers" ', in J.Fairbank (ed), *The Missionary Enterprise in China and America* (Cambridge, Mass., 1974), pp.197-225. Ma's baptismal name was Mathias.

54 A keen devotee of French Catholic education, Ma Xiangbo (Ma Liang) became principal of Zhendan University in 1903 and Fudan (Aurore) University in 1905. In 1913 he was appointed principal of Beijing University. He championed the use of a phonetic alphabet and the creation of an academy based on the model of the *Academie Française*.

55 The college had been established in 1850 and was originally known as the College of St.Ignatius. It was located in the residential home of Xu Guangqi (1562-1633), a prominent Ming dynasty official who had converted to Christianity. It was inherited by the Jesuits after Xu's death as a centre of missionary activity, but was closed down in 1773.

56 This was the first significant Chinese educational mission to Europe, although in 1866 three students from the Tongwenguan had spent three months in England and France, and in 1875 Giquel had taken five students with him when he returned to France to hire more specialists for the Fuzhou dockyard.

57 K.Biggerstaff, *The Earliest Modern Government Schools in China* (Ithaca, 1961), pp.75-76; S.Leibo, *Transferring Technology to China: Prosper Giquel and the Self-Strengthening Movement* (Berkeley, 1985), pp.126-128.

58 Established in 1872, the Ecole Libre des Sciences Politiques was reorganized as the Institut des Sciences Politiques after 1945. Until 1931 students without a *baccalauréat* could attend courses there.

59 Zeng Jize, who served as China's ambassador to France from 1879-1884, spoke highly of Ma's erudition. Chen Sanjing, 'Luelun Ma Jianzhong de waijiao sixiang', p.472.

60 C.Kim and H.Kim, *Korea and the Politics of Imperialism 1876-1910* (Berkeley, 1967), pp.20-28; M.Deuchler, *Confucian Gentlemen and Barbarian Envoys: The Opening of Korea 1875-1885* (Seattle, 1977), pp.116-122. See also Key-Hiuk Kim, *The Last Phase of the East Asian World Order* (Berkeley, 1980).

61 Ma is credited with inserting the preamble to the treaty in which the Korean king informed the US president of Korea's vassal status vis-a-vis China. By 1893 Korea had signed treaties with Britain, Italy, Russia, Germany and France.

62 The loan contract provided for 300,000 taels from the China Merchants Steam Navigation Company and 200,000 taels from the Kaiping Mining Company. As it turned out, only 200,000 taels were eventually lent. No repayment seems to have been made, except for a small reduction in 1891. M.Deuchler, *Confucian Gentlemen and Barbarian Envoys*, p.273, fn.3. See also L.Sigel, 'Business-Government Cooperation in Late Qing Korean Policy'.

63 Entitled *Ma shi wentong* (with an English title of 'Chinese Grammar For Middle Schools'), the first edition was published in Shanghai in 1904. A nineteenth edition was published in 1927. This was virtually the first work on Chinese grammar.

64 L.Sigel, 'Business-Government Cooperation in Late Qing Korean Policy'.

65 Such a policy entailed making Korea a virtual colonial dependency. There is an intriguing parallel here between the views of the comprador, Zheng Guanying, who in the 1870s argued that China's traditional policy of non-interference in the domestic affairs of tributary states be replaced by a more active one that advanced China's political and economic influence and those of Wei Yuan in the early nineteenth century advocating a more active maritime policy in Southeast Asia to preempt Western encroachment. The extent to which Western models of colonialism influenced Chinese reformers in the late nineteenth century (touched on in Sigel's essay noted above) is a fascinating question that awaits further research.

66 S.Mann, *Local Merchants and the Chinese Bureaucracy 1750-1950* (Stanford, 1987), p.147.

67 J.Ch'en, *State Economic Policies of the Ch'ing Government 1840-1895* (New York, 1980), p.56.

68 P.Cohen, *Between Tradition and Modernity: Wang T'ao and Reform in Late Ch'ing China*, p.16.

69 *ibid.*, pp.39-42, 65-66.

70 *ibid.*, pp.196, 205.

71 On Zheng Guanying's reform thought, see Hao Yen-p'ing, *The Comprador in Nineteenth Century China*, pp.197-205.

72 P.Cohen, *Between Tradition and Modernity: Wang T'ao and Reform in Late Ch'ing China*, pp.244-245 distinguishes three 'types' of reformers: those representing the 'extreme littoral' such as Tang Tingshu (1832-1892) who worked in the treaty ports and had no grounding in the classical Confucian education, those representing the hinterland, such as classically trained Xue Fucheng and Guo Songdao (1818-1891), who had little contact with the cosmopolitan culture of the treaty ports, and those who had ties with the littoral but who also had a grounding in Confucian education such as Ma Jianzhong, Wang Tao and Zheng Guanying.

73 Xue Fucheng served as Chinese Ambassador to Britain, France, Italy and Belgium from 1890 to 1894. His journals were published in sixteen volumes in 1892 and 1896. Excerpts from these journals have recently been translated by Helen Hsieh Chien, *The European Diary of Hsieh Fucheng: Envoy Extraordinary of Imperial China* (New York, 1993). For comments on Xue's 1879 reform proposals, see the introduction by D.Howland, pp.xiv-xvi. They have been partially translated in Wm. de Bary et. al., *Sources of Chinese Tradition* (New York, 1960), vol.2, pp.52-55.

74 Yen-p'ing Hao, 'Changing Chinese Views of Western Relations 1840-1895'. in J.Fairbank and Kwang-ching Liu (eds), *The Cambridge History of China, vol.11* (Cambridge, 1980) pp.188-190.

75 See Banno Masataka, *Chūgoku kindaika to Ba Kenchū*, pp.18-24.

76 See, for example, the journal of Li Shuchang (1837-1897), who served in the Chinese

embassies in London, Paris and Madrid before becoming Chinese Minister to Japan in 1881. Entitled *Xiyang Zazhi* (Random Notes on the West), it has been translated into French by Shi Kangqiang, *Carnet de Notes sur l'Occident* (Paris, 1988).

77 J.Frodsham, *The First Chinese Embassy to the West*, pp.xliii-xliv.

78 On the thought of Yan Fu, see B.Schwartz, *In Search of Wealth and Power: Yen Fu and the West* (Cambridge, Mass., 1964).

79 It is interesting to note that Ma's perhaps more realistic description of the British parliamentary system contrasted with that given by Western missionaries in China. W.Muirhead, for example, in an article published by the missionary journal *Wanguo gongbao* (Globe Magazine) in 1878, described the British political system as one in which ministers and officials were controlled (!) by an elected parliament. A.Bennett, *Missionary Journalist in China* (Athens, Georgia, 1983), pp.184-185.

80 Banno Masataka, 'Furansu ryūgaku jidai no Ba Kenchū' (Ma Jianzhong in France), *Kokka gakkai zasshi*, no.5 (August 1971), pp.258-291.

81 Ma was referring to the continued Western demand since 1860 that China send diplomats abroad. The Treaty of Tianjin (1860) had provided for the establishment of foreign diplomatic legations in Beijing.

82 For example, proposals to abolish footbinding often cited Western ridicule of Chinese customs.

83 The rolling stock and tracks were later transferred and used in Taiwan.

84 M.Wright, *The Last Stand of Chinese Conservatism*, pp.177-178.

85 Such popular fears of railroads were not unique to China. J.Ch'en, *State Economic Policies of the Ch'ing Government 1840-1895* (p.94) notes that the Liverpool-Manchester Railroad Bill was rejected in 1824 on the grounds that cows would be frightened by the noise and produce less milk, birds would be driven away by the smoke and sparks would set fire to houses.

86 R.Huenemann, *The Dragon and the Iron Horse: The Economics of Railroads in China 1876-1937* (Cambridge, Mass., 1984), p.5.

87 E.Carlson, *The Kaiping Mines 1877-1912* (Cambridge, Mass., 1971), p.19. Passenger traffic also began at this time. In 1883 the Kaiping Company imported three passenger coaches as well as fifty coal trucks.

88 An alternative line linking Hankou in central China with Lugouqiao on the outskirts of Beijing was approved of at this time, although funds for the project were eventually diverted to finance an extension of the Tangshan line north-eastwards beyond the Great Wall. R.Huenemann, *The Dragon and the Iron Horse*, pp.44-46. In 1891 a line was built between Taibei and Jilong (Keelung) in Taiwan, which was later extended to Xinzhu (Hsin-chu), a total of 66 miles.

89 In a letter to Li Hongzhang in 1877 Guo Songdao also recommended the building of railroads in China; like Ma he argued that they would bring officials and people together and prevent exploitation by local officials from being covered up. J.Frodsham, *The First Chinese Embassy to the West*, p.103. For a discussion of Ma's ideas on railroads, see Banno Masatake, *Chūgoku kindaika to Ba Kenchū*, pp.89-125; and Zhao Fengtian, *Wanqing wushi nian jingji sixiang shi* (A history of economic thought in the last fifty years of the Qing dynasty), Beiping, 1939, pp.155-159.

90 Zhang Zhidong's memorial is translated in J.Ch'en, *State Economic Policies of the Ch'ing Government 1840-1895*, pp.159-166. Zhang argued that railroads would facilitate the transport of goods, stimulate mining, and provide swift famine relief.

91 W.Chan, *Merchants,Mandarins and Modern Enterprise in Late Ch'ing China* (Cambridge, Mass., 1977), pp.85-87.

92 The social history of train travel in late nineteenth and early twentieth century China is a subject that awaits research. One intriguing question is to what extent political and social status distinctions were reinforced (or subverted) by such clear differentiation amongst passengers.

93 A.Feuerwerker, *China's Early Industrialization*, p.41. The Qing government began to resort to foreign loans on a much larger scale after 1895. Three loans totalling £47.8 million were contracted in 1895 to pay for the indemnity imposed on China after the Sino-Japanese War. The first sizeable railroad loans were contracted in 1898. Between 1899-1911 90% of foreign loans were used for building railroads; the price paid for such loans, however, was the bestowal of construction rights to foreign agencies as well as the granting of some monopoly power in the supply of construction materials. Hou Chi-ming, *Foreign Investment and Economic Development in China 1840-1937*, p.24.

94 The emphasis on the people (*min*) differed from that of another essay with a similar-sounding title written by the American missionary Young J.Allen in 1872 and published in *Wanguo gongbao* (Globe Magazine). Entitled *Zhiyi zhi lun: fuguo shuo* (On that which is most beneficial: the enrichment of the country) it recommended the exploitation of China's natural resources. Ma's emphasis was shared by Guo Songdao, who also maintained that state wealth and the prosperity of the people were inseparable. Yen-p'ing Hao, 'Changing Chinese Views of Western Relations 1840-1895', pp.171-172.

95 For analyses of Ma's 1890 essay, see Hayashi Yozo, 'Shinmatsu kairyōha Ba Kenchū: "fumin setsu" no keisei katei' (The late Qing reformer Ma Jianzhong and the development of the theory of 'enriching the people'), *Chūgokushi kenkyū*, no.1 (1962), pp.1-17; and Hayashi Yozo, 'Ba Kenchū keizai shisō: "fumin" shisō no seiretsu oyobi sono yakuwari' (The economic thought of Ma Jianzhong: the role of the concept of 'enriching the people'), *Tezukayama Daigaku kiyō*, no.2 (1966), pp.191-219.

96 In 1866-67 China had a total trade deficit of 26.9 million taels, although in 1872 and 1876 China enjoyed a trade surplus. By 1890, when Ma wrote his essay, the total value of imports had reached 128,758,000 taels while that of exports only totalled 88,809,289 taels. J.Ch'en, *State Economic policies of the Ch'ing Government 1840-1895*, p.210.

97 R.Gardella, *Harvesting Mountains*, pp.6, 62.

98 China's tea exports declined further to 184,530,000 lbs in 1900, while Indian tea exports for that year totalled 192,310,000 lbs. R.Gardella, *ibid.*, p.111. China also faced increasing competition from the plantation production of Ceylon and the Dutch East Indies.

99 R.Gardella, *ibid.*, p.132.

100 *ibid.*, p.136. One should note, however, that Japan's exports were greatly boosted after 1895 when it annexed Taiwan following the Sino-Japanese War.

101 R.Eng, *Economic Imperialism in China*, p.25.

102 L.Li, *China's Silk Trade*, pp.70-71.

103 *ibid.*, p.72.

104 *ibid.*, pp.74-75, 83-87.

105 R.Gardella, *Harvesting Mountains*, p.117. Interestingly, a proposal had been made as early as 835 by a Chinese official to transplant all tea shrubs to official plantations. The proposal was rejected because of potential opposition from growers. R.Gardella, *ibid.*, p.24.

106 R.Gardella, *ibid.*, p.95.

107 R.Eng, *Economic Imperialism in China*, pp.88-89 has noted a similar situation with regard to the silk trade. Each foreign export firm could conduct its own tests on the goods and its assessment could not be disputed by Chinese sellers. If the goods were returned the foreign firm was not responsible for costs or damages incurred during inspection. This inspection prerogative could be used to bargain for lower prices, especially as payment was only made when the goods were actually on board ship. Until then Chinese sellers had to continue

paying rent (for storage) and interest payments on loans.

108 M.Wright, *The Last Stand of Chinese Conservatism*, pp.167-168. The tax remained in force until 1931.

109 R.Gardella, *Harvesting Mountains*, p.93.

110 S.Mann, *Local Merchants and the Chinese Bureaucracy 1750-1950*, pp.146-147.

111 Most Chinese officials dreaded the prospect of treaty revision since it was assumed foreigners would use the opportunity to enhance even further their privileges in China. Ma viewed treaty revision as an opportunity to increase import duties and reduce export duties.

112 P.Cohen's description of the coastal or littoral reformers applies very well to Ma Jianzhong: 'Cosmopolitan in outlook, nationalists before their time, their attachment was less to Confucian values than to the Chinese nation'. *Between Tradition and Modernity*, pp.244-245.

113 A.Feuerwerker, *China's Early Industrialization*, pp.39-40 dismisses reformers such as Ma Jianzhong as woolly-headed thinkers with no influence to put their ideas into practice. J.Ch'en, *State Economic Policies of the Ch'ing Government*, p.2 compares Ma Jianzhong and others with French and British mercantilists of the 17th and 18th centuries, noting that they were hampered by an ignorance of economics and technology. Ma's writings indicate that Chinese 'mercantilists' were perhaps just as much concerned with improving people's livelihoods as with enhancing state wealth, and that they might not have been so ignorant of economics and technology as Chen supposes.

114 *Shike zhai jiyan jixing* (Recorded words and deeds from the Shike Studio), preface dated 1896; reprinted Taibei, n.d. Liang also noted in 1896 that Ma Jianzhong had taught him Latin. See Ding Wenjiang, Zhao Fengtian (comp), *Liang Qichao nianpu changbian* (A chronology of Liang Qichao's life),Shanghai, 1983, pp.51, 56-57.

115 W.Chan, *Merchants,Mandarins and Modern Enterprise in Late Ch'ing China*, pp.32-33.

116 R.Gardella, *Harvesting Mountains*, p.145. A state sponsored experimental tea station was also opened near Nanjing to investigate improved methods of tea cultivation.

117 L.Li,*China's Silk Trade*, pp.189-190.

118 W.Chan, *Merchants,Mandarins and Modern Enterprise in Late Ch'ing China*, p.226. Provincial governments also set up institutions of their own such as bureaux of commercial affairs, bureaux for the protection of merchants and bureaux of industry. *ibid.*, pp.201-204.

119 *ibid.*, pp.179-182.

A Letter to Li Hongzhang on Overseas Study (1878)[1]

A fter May I was extremely busy with my courses at the Ecole Libre des Sciences Politiques.[2] This, together with the fact that the examinations were fast approaching, meant I had no time to copy out my journal entries to send on to you. Also, in the last week of May Ambassador Guo Songdao arrived in France[3] and at the beginning of June he presented his diplomatic credentials. I then was asked to take up concurrently the posts of embassy translator and interpreter with a gratefully received increased salary. I dared not refuse such a generous offer from my superior. Moreover, the translation and interpreting duties have been few and have not taken up too much of my energies, and so I still have been able to carry out my original plans in coming to Europe.

The examinations took place during the last week of June. There were eight essay topics. The first one was: 'Based on a reading of the 1,800-page *Law of Nations*[4] discuss the disputed cases of diplomacy and war amongst the various nations that are still at issue.' The second one was: 'On the basis of the various international treaties discuss each country's foreign trade, deciphering procedures, telegraphic communications, railroads, weights and measures, currency, land use regulations, penal system and mediation procedures'. The third topic was: 'Based on the commercial legislation in various countries discuss the means whereby confidence is maintained in the bills of exchange issued by chambers of commerce.' The existence of such confidence enables one to realize very clearly that in the last one hundred years the source of Western prosperity does not lie solely in the pioneering use of machinery but rather, more importantly, in the protection of chambers of commerce on the one hand and in good laws and government on the other. The costs for railroads, telegraphs, steam-driven machinery and mining are enormous and therefore trust is of the essence so as to dispel worries that public support will not be forthcoming. Thus while gold and silver reserves might be limited the amount available for expenditure is inexhaustible because paper notes are used instead of bullion. Limited only by trust one copper coin in effect can serve the purposes of several hundred such coins.

The fourth topic was: 'The unofficial histories of various countries focus on the secret correspondence of diplomats and foreign ministries as a way of understanding such matters as Prussia's rise to hegemony, the unification of Russia, the entrenched bitterness between Russia and Turkey and the oscillating fortunes in the mutual rivalry of England and France. Thus you can proceed with a detailed exposition of the causes for these events.' The fifth topic was: 'What are the advantages and disadvantages of the different political systems of England, the US and France and of the ways in which rulers and ruled are brought together? Why is it that England's system has endured for a long time without changing, America's system has not undergone change but is getting worse and France's system has undergone repeated change but with no improvement?' The sixth topic was: 'In looking at the governing practices of Prussia, Belgium, Switzerland and Austria we see that Prussia has followed a policy of annexation, Switzerland a policy of federation, Belgium a policy of neutrality and Austria a policy of recovery after recent setbacks. Assess these countries' successes and failures in their ways of dealing with such matters.'

The seventh topic involved comments on the following

observations: 'Each country's constitution is very different; some are monarchies, some are republics, while others are constitutional monarchies. The legislative, executive and judicial powers are separated and are not monopolized by any one body.' It is very clear that since there are no mutual infringements of authority government affairs all fall smoothly into place. Top officials are not involved in tax collection; corrupt officials have no scope to indulge their personal ambitions; criminal charges are dealt with by local juries; and oppressive officials are unable to abuse the law. Everyone has individual autonomy and hence is imbued with a feeling of self-respect. The eighth topic was: 'In terms of tax regulations and government borrowing why is it that although taxes in Western countries are ten times more than those levied in China, the people are not resentful neither are they suspicious when the government seeks public loans?'

The examinations lasted three days; I used up at least twenty notebooks and wrote about one hundred paragraphs in total. My detailed answers all received top marks from the teachers and the assessment was published in the bulletin. It noted: 'A penetrating and subtle analysis that has brought out the essential points. Such answers cannot be compared to those that simply plough through outdated writings.' It has not been long since Westerners and Chinese have had dealings with each other and very often Westerners have looked down on us. Thus as soon as one of us shows some persipacity they offer exalted praise as if such merit is totally unexpected. Yet it is this very expression of surprise that belittles us. All I did was to study with determination for the examinations; I certainly would not dare to think highly of myself because of one minor success.

Since coming to Paris I have made contact with many people in authority, but the people with whom I get along the best are the so-called academicians.[5] They are specialists in mathematics, chemistry and other scientific subjects as well as in the evolution of government systems. They are esteemed by every country and highly respected. These learned scholars, seeing that I am embarked upon an investigation of Western knowledge, have sincerely given me advice. They all urged me to take the university entrance examinations and thus gain scholarly honour in their country.

I replied that I had come a long way to study in order to seek concrete knowledge rather than to gain a reputation. These scholars replied: 'We Westerners are also concerned with the potential harm of only competing for reputation instead of devoting oneself to acquiring concrete knowledge. However, if one's reputation is not widely recognized one's knowledge is not made widely known. Thus at the time Westerners and Chinese first came into contact the fact that sometimes the Chinese were taken advantage of was not because of their lack of knowledge or ability but rather because the fame of those with learning was not acknowledged and what they had studied was therefore not put to use. In such a situation the Chinese did not have the means to convince others of their learning. Now, the main requirements for the conduct of diplomacy are a knowledge of languages and legal principles, while the way to seek national wealth and strength lies in a knowledge of mathematics and science. China need not worry that it is not wealthy but rather that the sources of wealth are not being tapped. In the future colossal undertakings such as the opening of mines, the establishment of wine distilleries, the manufacture of machinery, the building of railroads and the erection of telegraph lines will all require knowledge of mathematics, chemistry and other general science subjects. In our country it is primarily a knowledge of these disciplines that brings scholarly honour. If you want to pursue practical studies you must concentrate on these subjects. With your current level of knowledge, if you pursue your studies further it will be very easy for you to gain scholarly success. Why should you fear this and not take the examinations?'

I discussed this conversation with my two supervisers, who allowed me to take the examinations. When I had finished the examinations on political science I took those on foreign languages and literature. They took place at the end of July and lasted two days. On the first day I drafted a Latin prose passage based on Emperor Augustus' edict to the subjugated Jews, as well as translating into French the Latin odes on the naval war between the Greeks and the Egyptians. The following day I was examined orally on geography and well-known Greek, Latin and French verse. In addition I had to answer questions on world history. I was again awarded top marks by the teachers, who expressed their wish to see French candidates attain my level. For a while in the ceremony hall there were several hundreds of people all applauding enthusiastically.

The news of my success was reported widely in the Paris newspapers, which noted that those coming to Paris to study from Japan, Persia and Turkey had all gained either the *baccalauréat* of science or a law diploma. There had not been anyone from Asia before me, the newspapers remarked, who had gained a *baccalauréat* of arts.[6] The fact that my modest success due to a limited amount of study provoked such a stir clearly reflects how obsessed Westerners are with fame. At the end of the year I will take the second stage of the exams for the *baccalauréat* of arts as well as taking the exams for the *baccalauréat* of science. Next spring and summer I may take the exams for the law diploma and higher science degree.

In recent days I have had a slight break from my studies and have visited the Paris Exhibition.[7] The streets of Paris are crowded with people and traffic from all over Europe, many times more than the norm. The new inventions of every country displayed by the Exhibition prompt people to come back time and again to marvel over them. Awards are given to the best displays in the hope of encouraging resourceful inventors. However, there are no new outstanding developments in military technology since no conclusive decisions have been reached over the relative merits and disadvantages of muzzle loading and breech loading cannon, or gun cotton and gun powder. Likewise, there is no consensus over whether the armour plating on ships should be horizontally or vertically welded, whether lighthouse lamps should rotate or remain stationery, whether water mines should be moored, fired or floated, and whether coastal batteries should be linked together, pointed at adjacent angles and be equipped with multiple or single barrels. Furthermore, in the mining industry it is still a matter for regret that no solution has yet been devised to prevent the spread of coal gas fumes that permeate mines and that no appropriate method has been found to operate elevator lifts to facilitate descent into the mines. In the textile industry the way to deal with such problems as machine-woven cotton cloth being easy to produce but not very durable, machine-pressed woollen cloth being durable but not smooth, and machine-spun silk being low-priced but not very shiny awaits further research. As for printing, winemaking and agricultural technology most of it draws on old designs displayed formerly at exhibitions in Austria and the US; no new machinery has yet been pioneered.

Also, the new inventions of the telephone and phonograph are simply novelties and ultimately have no great value.[8] The only novel items not seen before in exhibitions were the personal jewellry collection of the English Crown Prince and antique bronzes belonging to the French aristocracy. Yet such items were nothing more than a boastful and extravagant display for the amusement of visitors so as to allow the French to indulge their elevated self image. Surely this could not have been the original intention of opening the Exhibition! The French created this Exhibition not to dazzle the eyes with novelties, but to display their wealth. Following the payment of the indemnity after its defeat by Prussia, France has experienced difficulties in reviving its prosperity. The country is thus recently embarked on a quest for wealth and strength, and opened this Exhibition especially to show off its wealth to foreigners.

It was said that there were some important things missing from the Chinese display. Thus although silk and tea are major Chinese products there was no display of the different silks produced by China's provinces nor of the different varieties of Chinese teas. It was also said that the ceramics on display were not very old and that the embroidery was not refined or of a high quality; neither had a single redeeming feature. It was also said that the agricultural implements and wax figures on display all resembled mere toys. It would seem that mighty China ultimately could not even match up to the islands of Japan. Can it be that this was because the management of Japan's display was entrusted to the Japanese themselves, whereas the organization of China's display was entrusted to Westerners? Looking at the way Westerners displayed China's products we can see how shallow is their knowledge of China. Someone asked me about this but I could only reply that since there was a Chinese supervisor of the display I dared not transgress his authority and give my own detailed views on the matter. Anyway, these are my general observations on the Paris Exhibition.

When recalling the year or so since I came to Europe I remember that originally I assumed Europe's wealth and strength solely lay in its highly developed manufacturing industry and in its strict military discipline. When I delved further into its laws and examined its arts of government I realized that Europe's search for wealth had as its basis the protection of commercial organizations and that its quest for strength had as its guiding principle the gaining of popular support. By protecting commercial organizations taxes can be increased, thereby ensuring state revenues are sufficient; by gaining popular support loyalty and devotion are increased manyfold, thereby ensuring shared hatred of external enemies. Other important aspects of European civilization such as the establishment of schools to increase daily the number of educated people, the opening of parliaments to allow public opinion to be expressed, the spread of manufacturing industry and the build-up of armies and navies are all offshoots of these two basic features. I therefore thought that the countries of Europe had perfect ways of governing. However, when I attended courses at the Ecole Libre des Sciences Politiques and taken in the responses to my repeated enquiries addressed to the learned gentlemen there, I finally realized that the idea of not believing everything one reads in books had a certain validity.[9]

England has a monarch and a bicameral parliament, which seem to be the centre of government. It is not known, however, that the monarchy merely signs its assent to laws, while parliament merely engages in empty talk. The levers of real political power are in the hands of the prime minister and one or two of his close cabinet ministers. Whenever there is a crisis they avoid responsibility and say it is up to parliament to deal with it. The American president is elected by the people and it would appear that he is devoted to public service rather than personal gain. However, everytime there is an election bribery is openly practised. With a change of president there is a change of governing personnel; incoming officials are all members of the new president's clique. How can such people be trusted to govern the country! France is a republic and it seems that those who enter government do not come from the ranks of the aristocracy. Yet people do not realize that such officials form tightly-knit factions. With the exception of capable and outstanding figures such as Thiers,[10] it is difficult for people to acquire high office or posts. Similar examples of this kind are too numerous to list.

Since looking into the political affairs of each country, although I have as yet been unable to penetrate the inner intricacies, I have grasped the main outlines. I am thinking of compiling my observations in a written work to be entitled *An Enquiry Into Government*, which will not only contain details gained from my reading but also information I have heard in conversation. Such a work, I believe, will be of benefit. Westerners consider profit or gain as the starting point for everything. I would therefore first write about exploiting sources of wealth; then, in the following order, I would write about improving the people's livelihood; enhancing state revenues; perfecting the standards of officialdom; widening the channels of communication between rulers and ruled; establishing a rigorous examination system; improving military and civil administration; and, finally, seeking ways to encourage international communication. I have already put together a small collection of observations but I regret that my knowledge is so meagre and that my reading has not been very wideranging. As a result I am often unable to express my exact meaning in words. All I can do is to record what I have learnt so as not to be unworthy of your trust in me on the one hand, and to remind people of the fundamentals of Western learning on the other. May I therefore take the liberty of presenting my humble views?

NOTES

1   The letter is dated 1877 in both Ma Jianzhong, *Shike zhai jiyan jixing* (Recorded words and deeds from the Shike Studio), reprint, Taibei, n.d., and Ma Jianzhong, *Shike zhai jiyan* (Recorded words from the Shike Studio), Beijing, 1960. Internal evidence shows that it must have been written in 1878. See Banno Masataka, *Chūgoku kindaika to Ba Kenchū*, p.24. The letter is also reprinted in Zhongguo shixue hui (comp.), *Yangwu Yundong* (Shanghai, 1962), vol.1, pp.425-429.

2   Ma attended the Ecole Libre des Sciences Politiques from November 1877 to June 1878 and again from November 1878 to June 1879. Banno Masataka, *Chūgoku kindaika to Ba Kenchū*, p.19.

3   Guo Songdao had been appointed Chinese Ambassador to Britain in 1877. In 1878 he took up the concurrent post of Chinese Minister to France. After his recall in 1879 he was succeeded by Zeng Jize (the son of Zeng Guofan), who remained in the post until 1884.

4   Ma is probably referring here to Henry Wheaton's *Elements of International Law*, originally published in 1836 and translated into Chinese for the Tongwenguan by W.A.P.Martin, an American missionary in China and interpreter for the US mission there. Its Chinese title was *Wanguo gongfa* (Public Law of all Nations), which is the title Ma uses in his letter. See I.Hsu, *China's Entrance into the Family of Nations: The Diplomatic Phase 1858-1880* (Cambridge, Mass., 1960), pp.125-131. Other works of international law translated into Chinese under the auspices of the Tongwenguan inclued de Martens' *Guide Diplomatique*, Bluntschli's *Droit International Codifié*, and the *Code Napoleon*. K.Biggerstaff, *The Earliest Modern Government Schools in China* (Ithaca, 1961), pp.152-153.

5   Ma is referring here to the members of the *Academie Française*, which he translates as *hanliyuan*. The Hanliyuan, in fact, was the Imperial Academy in Beijing, a government institution in which the most outstanding Confucian scholars researched and lectured on the Classics.

6   This particular section of Ma's letter has been partially translated in Y.C.Wang, *Chinese Intellectuals and the West 1872-1949* (Chapel Hill, 1966), pp.80-81.

7   The Paris Exhibition was opened in 1878. There were further exhibitions in 1889 and 1900.

8   Both Bell's telephone and Edison's phonograph were displayed at the Exhibition. Ma was apparently not the only one to express scepticism. The Selection Committe of the Exhibition's electrical section almost refused to accept Bell's invention since they regarded it as a toy and even a fraud. E.Weber,France: *Fin de Siècle* (Cambridge, Mass., 1986), p.74.

9   Ma quotes here from Mencius: 'If one believed everything in the Book of History (*Shu jing*), it would have been better for the Book not to have existed at all' (*jin xin Shu ze buru wu Shu*). The *Shu jing* was one of the early Confucian classics. See D.C.Lau (trans), *Mencius* (Harmondsworth, 1970), p.194.

10 Adolphe Thiers (1797-1877), journalist, historian and politician. He became the first President of the Third Republic in 1871.

Reply from Marseille to a Friend (1878)[1]

I have received your esteemed letter asking me to draw up regulations for a diplomats' college that will be appropriate to China's situation. I think that sending diplomatic envoys abroad to every country has required hundreds of thousands in government expenditures.[2] It does not benefit the state, but rather is a measure that has been forced upon the court. Sending diplomats abroad is simply opening up a new official career path suitable only for those who intend to achieve personal gain. Now, all those who claim to have some understanding of contemporary affairs often remark: 'The basic strategy lies in seeking wealth and strength through exploiting mineral resources, building ironworks, erecting coastal defences and protecting strategic passes. In this way state coffers will be full and military strength will daily be enhanced. We will then be able to face down Europe and who would not be in awe of us! Sending diplomats abroad is simply engaging those skilled at negotiating in particular circumstances. How can this be spoken of in the same breath as implementing a basic strategy?' However, people have been mouthing these words for the last ten years or more and yet mines have not been sunk, and iron ore still lies untouched in the ground. As for cannon emplacements and gunboats, some are unsuitable and cannot be used while others that can be used have not as yet been organized into a cohesive force. By way of contrast our diplomats are to be found all over Europe.

Thus up until today the so-called basic strategy has not been carried out whereas, paradoxically, a so-called secondary measure *has* been implemented in the wake of foreign pressure. In terms of what we need to do now we should take the initiative and come up with an approach to this so-called less urgent policy that has been originally forced upon us by others; in other words it is better to do something later than never[3] to turn the situation to our advantage. What might be such an approach? I would say that it is simply ensuring the rigorous selection of diplomatic talent. How is this to be done? It is simply a matter of providing the proper training.

The foreigners' wish that we send diplomatic envoys to their countries has two purposes in mind. Firstly, if Chinese diplomats are stationed in foreign capitals whenever there is an important ceremony they will, along with other foreign diplomats, line up in accordance with their rank to offer their respectful congratulations. The presence of such diplomats will provide the occasion with an impressive aura. Our diplomats will therefore be nothing more than adornments to bring prestige to the host country. Secondly, Westerners love to flaunt their achievements. In the last one hundred years their political systems have undergone extensive change, commerce has spread and provided more opportunities for earning a livelihood, and parliaments have been established to allow expression of public opinion. Thus taxes are always reported and paid in full and there are no worries about embezzlement of government revenues; legal judgements tally with the facts and are equitable; and degrading corporal punishment is not practised. People live and work in contentment and tranquility; everyone gets on with what they are supposed to do without interference from others. Although Western people are not as deeply content as they would be under the rule of a true king they are a little more cheerful than they would be under the rule of a feudal lord.[4] The streets and thoroughfares are kept clean and tidy, the road surfaces smooth and even; there is no need for a street watchman and people do not have to lock their doors at night. Such phenomena are the effects rather than the basic causes of Western wealth and strength.

Westerners, nevertheless, all like to boast about these things and often remark: 'Even after four thousand years of culture and learning China has not yet been able to reach the stage we have achieved,whereas we in the last one hundred years have done away with outmoded ideas and practices so that we have daily prospered and attained our current state of well-being'. They therefore want Chinese scholars to acquire a deeper understanding of Western culture so as to bring about rapid improvements. What better way to achieve this, they feel, than having Chinese diplomats live amongst them,[5] observing, and learning from, the Western way of life day and night? Westerners assume that in the future such diplomats will be teachers when they return to China and thus will not betray the hopes of those neighbourly countries who had received them. So although foreign countries insist that we send envoys abroad out of an extravagant wish to show off, they are still quite happy to do so.

Our diplomats, on assuming their position and as soon as they have delivered their credentials and introductory speech, are quite content just to fulfill their official duties conscientiously without doing anything improper. Perhaps they might attend a formal banquet in their host capitals decked out in ceremonial dress, but they do not stay long and quickly retire to their residences, having no contact with anyone. Even when they do interact socially it is usually with social climbers and hangers-on, so that guests visiting their official residences are for the most part of the vulgar and mediocre kind, lacking in education and *savoir-faire*. Westerners, therefore, consider Chinese diplomats as figures of fun and do not think people from Asia are worth talking to. Some might say: 'Since the educational level of countries such as Turkey and Egypt is not very advanced it is not surprising that they do not understand the conventions of international diplomacy. The Japanese, also, have the nature of circus monkeys; they imitate others without distinguishing between wisdom and foolishness or between fundamental and trivial matters. Their tradition of learning is also more recent than ours, so it is no wonder they do not have a deep understanding of others. But China is a country that Westerners have always looked up to, and is a country with a four thousand year-old culture. Yet today, when our diplomats arrive at their posts with official titles such as counsellor or attaché, even though they perform all the ritual niceties such as presenting their credentials and making eulogistic addresses, no-one has the slightest interest in asking them about such important matters as our country's system of government, education, economy, laws and military capabilities. Perhaps their foreign hosts know about these things and do not deign to inquire further, or perhaps they are ignorant of such matters but pretend boastfully they are not. Could it be also that they despise those we send to engage in international intercourse, or that they simply lump our representatives along with those from Turkey, Persia and Japan? With such closed minds it is as if our diplomats were still in China.' I think it would be a great pity if we used these observations to argue that sending diplomats abroad is unimportant.

On the contrary, I would argue that these drawbacks do not mean that the policy of sending diplomats abroad is unwise and should not be carried out. Rather they are the result of not appointing the right people for the job and not training them properly. Titles such as counsellor and attaché are simply traded as personal gifts to lubricate the official system and those who acquire them are not qualified to manage public affairs. Those who do acquire such titles consider themselves lucky and simply plan on accumulating several years worth of salary so that in the future they can enjoy an ostentatious life-style. If they have to embark on concrete training they study foreign languages. However, just when they are beginning to pronounce foreign words their term of duty has already expired and they have to rush back to China as ignorant as when they first went abroad.[6] What they call foreign affairs is simply a record of their journey from China to the West and various unseemly phenomena such as women's low-cut and sleeveless dresses that expose the neck and shoulders.[7] Even those who are slightly more aware of important matters can only remark: 'The way of government in the West lies generally in emphasizing profit through the promotion of mutual trust.' Yet when one inquires further as to the reasons why profit is emphasized and mutual trust promoted they can only dig out a few scattered anecdotes to serve as an illustration. They are completely at a loss to explain the fundamental causes of such an outlook. Alas! Was this really the original intention of the court when it bestowed these elevated posts with high paying salaries and especially opened up this new career path? We should carefully ponder the reasons why such a situation has inevitably come about despite original intentions.

Before the Zhou and Qin dynasties[8] sending diplomatic envoys to the far reaches of the earth was unheard of. Yet beginning with the edicts of Emperor Han Wudi[9] it was deemed proper to refer to envoys in the same breath as generals and ministers. We can thus see how important they must have been! Their intelligence, courage and resourcefulness had to be exceptional; their urbanity and wide learning had to be sufficient so as to cope with any situation; they had to be serene and broadminded so as always to act in accordance with etiquette. They also had to be sensitive to people's feelings and be aware of changes in any situation; they had to perform their duties with consummate skill, focusing on the key issues so as to solve problems easily.[10] They had to be thoroughly aware of any differences that might crop up at the beginning and to clearly perceive at the outset any beneficial or harmful trends. Only then would they be satisfied in having competently performed their duties.

Dong Zhongshu said that seeking out sages without first training scholarly talent is like seeking an exquisite piece of jade that has not been carved or polished.[11] Although diplomatic talent is prized in the West it is still difficult to think of more than a few exceptional individuals such as Bismarck, Talleyrand and Palmerston who have appeared in the last one hundred years. Now, the Chinese since ancient times have not had much contact with foreigners and have never studied the histories and languages of foreign countries. To assume that as soon as they have crossed the ocean our envoys will acquire an extensive knowledge of foreign government, learning and customs is rather like expecting a baby who is just gurgling his first words to tap to musical rhythms or to expect a baby crawling on its knees to behave in a dignified manner. In such a situation one might have books and the stern discipline of teachers on hand but ultimately they cannot be put to use. Is it because they do not have the will to respond to such guidance? No, it is simply a matter of insisting people perform a task for which they are not qualified or of being quick to criticize those who have not been given the appropriate training.

So what should be done? I would say that people like to share in success but it is more difficult to involve them in the initial planning of something. What I refer to as the appropriate assessment of talent and the implementation of rigorous training does not initially have to be some lofty and difficult task that will astonish the world. Rather if we look at what has already been achieved by the *Tongwenguan* and other foreign language schools today[12] we can see that results have been achieved simply by making use of limited resources, making the necessary adjustments to bring improvement and providing the appropriate instruction. I therefore propose the establishment of a college in Shanghai that will recruit intelligent sons (aged between 15 and 21 or 22 years) from good family backgrounds who have already completed study of the Five Classics and Four Books and have some rudimentary literary talent.

At the time they are recruited they should be given a written essay examination, either elucidating the meaning of part of a well known official memorial or arguing against its premises. The main purpose would be to test the candidate's ability to express his ideas clearly and fluently. Each year ten students would be recruited and the training would last three years. In the first year students would study French and Latin, in the second year literature and in the third year poetry. A certain standard would be expected at the end of each year. In addition to these regular courses students would still have to study Chinese history so that neither Western nor Chinese learning is over-emphasized. They should also at some time be provided with a rudimentary knowledge of foreign history, mathematics and science so that in the future they will be adept in social intercourse. At the end of each year there would be examinations; inferior students will be expelled from the course while the superior ones will be allowed to continue into the next year.

After the end of the three year course students completing the final overall examinations will have their dossiers sent to the Zongli Yamen,[13] and will either work as functionaries in China or be sent abroad as diplomatic attachés. The arrangement would last one year, and during this time each former student would still have to study English and the main outlines of French law to prepare them for the next two years of study. On completion of this probationary year trainees will be examined by their superiors in the embassy and then sent to a training school to be attached to our embassy in Paris to study for a further two years on the model of the consular translation section that the English have created within their legation in Beijing. On entering the training school students will be orally examined on what they have learnt during their probationary year in order to sort out the stronger and weaker candidates. Those who do not come up to standard will be ordered to repeat their studies, while those who do will be allowed to proceed with the two years of formal learning at the training school. During these two years they will be familiarized with written documents (in French and Chinese) on international law, legal cases, treaties, finance, taxes and international relations, as well as studying English and German. On completion of the two years their final examination results will be reported to the Zongli Yamen. Some trainees will then be appointed as officials within China, while others will be formally posted abroad with the rank of counsellor third class.

In this way, after six years of the appropriate training, although trainees will only have a general and rudimentary knowledge of Western learning they will at least have achieved the beginnings of a firm basis for the future. Moreover, before being promoted trainees will be tested on what they write and say; afterwards, when they are promoted to second class counsellors, first class counsellors and consuls, they will be assessed on their actions. Thus during the six years in which trainees proceed from being students to counsellors their character and talent will always be clearly evident. During their initial three years instruction trainees will be subject to the discipline of school regulations in order to temper their high spirits; in their probationary year restrictions will be relaxed in order to assess their self-control. Also, making them work in the embassy during their more relaxed probationary year will mould their characters and reform their youthful habits of impulsiveness and excessive haughtiness.

As a result of a further generous two years specializing in Western learning according to a strictly supervised curriculum trainees will be modest and unassuming in outlook but will have the wherewithal to achieve success. The misuse of talent will therefore be avoided. To select only ten student trainees every year and make them undergo six years of study before they are ready for employment may not amount to much. However, within ten years, when attitudes have been broadened and scholarly customs have changed, not only will it be invalid to decry the lack of talent in the Zongli Yamen but also it will not be impossible that trainees working abroad, having undergone extra study of Confucian learning in addition to performing their regular duties (thus providing them with the correct basics of thought and practice), might one day in the future be recalled to China to assist with government affairs.

What I have proposed is the initiative we must take now to deal with a government policy that was originally considered of secondary importance. There is no other alternative. As for the funds to support my proposed two training schools, I see no reason why we should not let our embassies abroad get rid of personnel who received their appointments simply by good fortune and make use of their salaries to cover the expenses. In this way we will have achieved after ten years the cultivation of real talent without the state having to fork out extra funds. Why should we therefore be hesitant and not implement my proposals?

NOTES

1   According to Banno Masataka, *Chūgoku kindaika to Ba Kenchū*, p.34 the letter was addressed to one of Li Hongzhang's associates and was meant to be read by officials at the Zongli Yamen.

2   By this time Chinese embassies had been opened in London, Berlin, Paris, Tokyo and Washington.

3   The phrase Ma uses here, *bulao guquan*, is drawn from the *Zhanguo ce* (Intrigues of the Warring States), a collection of anecdotes about interstate diplomacy during the late Zhou period (5th to 3rd centuries B.C) and which was probably compiled in the 2nd century B.C. *Bulao guquan* means to call on the hound only after seeing the hare, and to repair the pen only after the sheep has bolted; it has come to mean that it is never too late to do something; there is always something to be done to make up for lost time or past mistakes. The full citation is *jian tu er gu quan, wei wei wan ye; wang yang er bu lao wei wei chi ye* (to call for the hound only after seeing the hare cannot be considered as too late; to mend the pen after the sheep has bolted cannot be considered as too tardy). See *Zhongguo chengyu da cidian* (Shanghai, 1987), p.457.

4   Ma is alluding to a passage from Mencius: 'The people under a leader of the feaudal lords are happy; those under a true king are expansive and content.' D.C.Lau (trans), *Mencius*, p.184.

5   Lit: 'having Chinese diplomats live in Zhuang and Yue'. Ma is drawing on a passage from Mencius in which he asserted that if a councillor of Chu wanted his son to speak the language of Qi it would be appropriate for him to be sent to live in Zhuang and Yue (places in Qi). D.C.Lau (trans), *Mencius*, p.111.

6   Ma uses a phrase from the 3rd century A.D. work *Sanguozhi* (History of the Three Kingdoms). *Wu xia A Meng* has come to mean an untutored or ignorant person. See *Hanyu chengyu kaoshi cidian* (Beijing, 1989), p.1184.

7   The low-cut dresses of Western women often aroused the horror of Chinese diplomats. See, for example, Liu Xihong's observations of a ball he attended in London, in J.Frodsham, *The First Chinese Embassy to the West*, pp.139-140. Japanese envoys were equally scandalized by the 'lewdness' of Western women. See Masao Miyoshi, *As We Saw Them: The First Japanese Embassy to the West* (Berkeley, 1979), p.71.

8   Zhou Dynasty (1122 B.C.-256 B.C); Qin Dynasty (221 B.C.-207 B.C.).

9   Emperor Wudi of the Han dynasty (202 B.C.-220 A.D.) reigned from 141 to 87 B.C. He pursued an active foreign policy, subjugating southern Manchuria and most of Korea, and made extensive use of envoys to form alliances with non-Chinese peoples in central Asia in order to confront the military threat of the Xiongnu, nomadic tribes on the northern frontiers.

10   *pi xi dao kuan*. Ma quotes here from *Zhuangzi* ('yangsheng zhu' section) in which Butcher Ting explains to Lord Wenhui how he splits an ox: 'Relying upon the natural arrangement of its body I strike the big cavities and pass through the large crevices (*pi daxi dao dakuan*)'. It has come to mean the skilful and adroit performance of a task. See J.Ware (trans), *The Sayings of Chuang Chou* (New York, 1963), p.29; *Hanyu chengyu kaoshi cidian* (Beijing, 1989), p.775.

11   Dong Zhongshu (ca.179-104 B.C.) was a prominent Confucian scholar during the Han dynasty. The quote Ma uses can be found in Dong Zhongshu's biography (*zhuan* 56) in the *Han Shu* (Shanghai, 1962), vol.6, p.2512.

12   The *Tongwenguan*, known as the College of Foreign Languages or the Interpreters' College, was established in Beijing in 1862. The original intention was to train interpreters so that Chinese officials would not be dependent on foreign experts. By 1866 astronomy and mathematics had been added to the curriculum. It also sponsored the translation of

Western works on international law, economics, chemistry and physics. Similar schools of foreign languages were opened in Shanghai (1863), Canton (1864) and Fuzhou (1866). In 1902 the *Tongwenguan* was absorbed into the Imperial University, which had been set up in 1898. I.Hsu, *The Rise of Modern China*, pp.270-271.

13   The full name of this government institution was *Zongli geguo shiwu yamen* (Office for the general management of affairs with various countries). Established in 1861 specifically to handle relations with the Western powers, it has been described as a proto-foreign office, although it was always subordinate to the Grand Council. I.Hsu, *The Rise of Modern China*, pp.268-269.

A Discussion of Railroads (1879)[1]

There are some who say that the railroad originated in England while others say Germany, but for the time being I will not pursue this question further. What *can* be said is that the construction of roughly made iron tracks to accommodate wheels, thereby facilitating transportation and dispensing with animal power, first occurred in 1825 in the vicinity of coal mines in England. Thereafter, during the next twenty-four years, America, Austria, France, Belgium, Germany, Russia, Italy and Spain, fearing they would fall behind, all rushed to build railroad tracks of their own. By 1875, the first year of the Emperor Guangxu,[2] there were 136,298 miles[3] of railroad track in Europe. Of this total, England possessed 26,472 miles, France 26,298 miles, Germany 25,772 miles, Austria 16,238 miles and Russia 17,733 miles. Other countries such as Italy, Spain, Belgium, Sweden, Holland, Turkey and Switzerland all have at least 1,000 miles of railroad track. North and South America possess a total of 136,085 miles of railroad track, of which 116,874 have been laid in the United States. Today British India has over 10,000 miles of railroad track; in the north the railway extends beyond Nepal to Ngari in Tibet.[4] Railroads in Russia also wind their way more than one thousand *li*[5] east of the Urals and in the southeast have penetrated the grasslands of the Kazakhs.

During the last fifty years, in all countries of the world which have forged communications by land and water there is not one in which railways have not played a crucial role. The railroad has facilitated the convenient and rapid movement of military personnel, the transportation of grain supplies, the despatch of famine relief and the transfer of supplies from wealthier regions to less well-off ones. The sheer convenience of railroad transportation has dispelled worries about the effects of floods, drought and banditry, as well as preventing fluctuations in the price of grain. Consequently, countries that estimated their revenues to be either in the thousands or millions before they built railroads all could reckon on an income totalling either millions or billions once railroads had been built. This is because trains travel as fast as lightning or a whirlwind. They can transport huge amounts of material to distant places and cover thousands of *li* as if it were next door. In the past long-distance mail took several weeks to reach its destination; now the time can be calculated in hours. In the past journeys by water or land might take several months; now one arrives before the journey has hardly begun. Also, whereas previously several decades of tax administration did not guarantee constant revenues, now in less than a few months the state coffers often enjoy a surplus. Thus there is no other way to establish the basis for wealth and strength than to build railways. There are innumerable measures to be undertaken with regard to this endeavour, but all can be subsumed under three general headings: fundraising, construction, and management. Let me outline each in turn.

An enormous amount of capital has to be mobilized in order to begin building railroads, so obviously the most important priority is to raise the funds. Such funds can be sought from merchants, the government, or from government and merchants working in partnership. If merchants invest the capital themselves then they sell the shares and set up the railway companies without any government interference. The problem with this system is that merchant-run companies all compete for the market by lowering their freight charges, the result being that they become unprofitable and have to close down. England and America both carry out this method and if we look at the period from 1875 to 1877 (the first three years of Emperor Guangxu's reign), we see that 196 railway companies went bankrupt. If the government assumes responsibility then officials supervise the enterprise, ensuring that work is not begun on useless lines; furthermore the railroads that are built tend to be for the purpose of transporting troops rather than carrying out domestic trade. Germany and Russia have, to some extent, adopted this approach. Perhaps also officials might first be responsible for building railroads and then hand them over to private management, or the reverse might happen with private capital initiating railroad construction and then officials taking over the management. Germany is experimenting with this approach, which serves both military and commercial purposes.

However, if profits are unlikely to compensate for construction and management costs there is the method of officials and merchants assuming joint responsibility. France carries out this method, with Germany and Austria seeking to emulate it. The method consists in government leasing land to private entrepreneurs, using potential profits rather than the land's value to determine the duration of the lease. When the lease expires the land is returned to government ownership. Construction and management of the railroad is in private hands, although the government may provide subsidies. If merchant share capital is not sufficiently forthcoming the government may offer to pay the interest on share dividends itself in order to encourage investment. On the other hand, if the required capital to start the enterprise is so enormous that it is difficult to raise loans because of a lack of public confidence, the government may act as official guarantor; officials and merchants working closely together draw up the loan agreements and regulations. In sum, all these strategies are nothing more than simply adopting appropriate measures to suit particular situations and to ensure as much as possible that income exceeds expenditure.

Some will say: 'Official assistance to merchants will result in the expenditure of hundreds of millions of *taels*[6] and we worry that this will represent a serious drain on government reserves'. They do not know that although in 1875 (the first year of

Emperor Guangxu's reign) the French government's annual subsidy to railway companies totalled 40 million francs, the taxes on railway transport for that year amounted to 127 million francs and that, moreover, savings made in despatching mail and transporting troops amounted to 56 million francs. Thus in a year the government gained 183 million francs. Other countries might well learn from France's example.

Once the question of funds is settled the next matter to consider is the actual building of the railroad. This involves surveying the terrain, laying the tracks, manufacturing the trains and erecting stations. Since the terrain has to be even and the route convenient for travel, it is best to locate the track near well populated villages and towns and alongside rivers, where the ground is flat and moist. If this cannot be done and the track has to cross mountainous terrain then valleys should be sought in which to lay the track and the gradient should not exceed one in twenty. The steepness of those railways in America that exceed this gradient make travelling difficult and we should not follow that example. If a mountain proves to be an obstacle then it can be tunnelled from above to a depth of no more than twenty metres;[7] otherwise it is better to tunnel from the side. Mont Blanc tunnel, which joins France and Italy, is 12,000 metres in length. Depending on whether the rock was hard or soft, every three feet tunnelled at Mont Blanc involved costs ranging from 700 to 2,600 francs on top of expenditures for machinery. Gorges can be filled, again as long as they do not exceed twenty metres in length; otherwise it is better to buld bridges across them. Bridges that cross large rivers should be raised so as to enable river traffic to pass under. The costs in building such bridges are difficult to estimate. Where the track intersects with the public thoroughfare barriers should be set up and attendants posted. The attendant should close the barriers when a train is about to pass so as to prevent road traffic from crossing the line.

Railtracks are generally made from steel or iron. Steel can withstand wear and tear and is much superior to iron. The only problem is that steel tends to be more expensive, although it is nevertheless widely used today; the two most common methods for producing steel are those associated with Bessemers and Siemens. Railroad tracks are shaped like the character for *gong* (工), with some raised at the top and bottom to facilitate convenient use and others protruding at the top to allow wooden beams to be nailed across them. These are the easiest and most appropriate types to use since railroad tracks tend to alter shape slightly with time and it is not possible to change them. The wooden beams that span the track must be sturdy. The most durable type of wood is either fir or pine coated with creosote. The coating of each beam costs about one franc. Beams should not be more than five *chi*[8] in length, seven or eight *cun*[9] in width, and five or six *cun* thick. When laying the beams across the track they should be covered with small stones. The stones should be strong enough to bear heavy loads as well as arranged to allow air to pass through, thereby preventing the wood from decaying. Railroads can be either dual or single track. Double-line tracks are 1.3 *zhang* in width, while single-line tracks are seven *chi* in width. The gauge width is determined by the distance between wheels on either side of the engine. Train wheels in England are two French *chi*[10] apart. In other countries wheels are generally 1.5 *chi* apart, although in Russia it is sometimes 1.8 *chi*. The distance between wooden beams is determined by the length of each section of the track. Thus if it is six French *chi*, seven beams are laid down. Germany in the past has used cast-iron tracks with built-in beams but they have deteriorated and are difficult to change, so they are gradually being abandoned today. There are many other aspects to railroad construction which cannot be discussed here. What should be noted is that for every mile of railroad built the land costs 6,000 francs, bridge construction costs about 8,000 francs, the tracks and beams 5,000 francs and miscellaneous expenses 4,000 francs. Altogether the cost of building one mile of railroad comes to 23,000 francs. This represents the most economical estimate for single-track lines in each country. If it is a double-track line the cost is doubled, and if the line traverses high mountains and large rivers the costs are further increased.

There are different kinds of train. Those that have limited

horsepower but move quickly just carry passengers; those that have considerable horsepower but move slowly just carry freight. The speed of those trains that carry both passengers and freight varies. Passenger trains can travel between 80 and 160 miles in an hour. The wheels of a passenger train are large but the crankshaft is short, thus driving the wheel faster. One revolution of a large wheel is equivalent to several revolutions of a smaller wheel, and covers a little over two French *chi*. The train thus travels quickly. Since the crankshaft on such trains is short, however, the engine's horsepower is not great and therefore the train cannot pull heavy loads. Depending on its capacity each passenger train costs between 42,000 and 55,000 francs. The wheels of freight trains are small and the crankshaft is long, giving the train more horsepower. With smaller wheels freight trains move slowly, each revolution of the wheel covering just over one French *chi*. In one hour such trains do not travel more than 60 miles, although they can carry loads of up to 28,000 piculs.[11] A freight train can cost 117,000 francs. The wheel revolution of trains that carry both freight and passengers covers 1.5 French *chi* and such trains cannot travel more than 100 miles in an hour. Such trains cost 50,000 francs. The minimum number of engine wheels is four, although some trains have six, eight or even twelve. In all cases, however, only two wheels actually move. The moving wheels can be in the front or the back, while the funnels can be placed along the side or the middle of the engine. In the world of today changes are occurring all the time, so that the form of train transport never stays the same. Nevertheless, we can say that generally all trains perform the three functions mentioned above.

Passengers travel by first, second or third class. Each train has three kinds of wagon with the first class wagon having twenty-four seats, the second class forty seats and the third class fifty seats. First class wagons cost 10,000 francs, while second and third class wagons do not cost more than 6,000 francs each. Freight wagons cost from 800 to 3,000 francs. The style of passenger train wagons can vary from country to country; some may have additional sleeper carriages for the use of night travellers. These sleeper carriages are the most expensive of all, costing about 13,000 francs each. Passenger trains can draw twenty wagons while freight trains can draw thirty. Wagons are joined together from end to end, winding their way along the track like an awesome dragon circling the skies.

There are certain places where approaching trains stop and stations built for the convenience of embarking and disembarking passengers; waiting rooms are provided for those passengers remaining at the station. In the vicinity of the station there are water tanks to supply the steam furnaces and coal mines to provide plentiful stockpiles of fuel. Stations also have telegraph offices to receive and send information, inspection bureaux to tax goods and prevent smuggling, accountancy offices to receive payment and issue tickets, sheds and warehouses to house trains and store goods. Finally, there are signals to ensure that trains enter the sheds in an orderly way. Train stations can be as elaborate as the planners want, although the difference in cost would be enormous.

Once construction is underway it is then appropriate to deal with the question of management. Train stations can be divided into first, second or third class depending on how busy they are. Such a distinction determines the kind of management structure. Each station should have a general manager in overall charge, an accountant to check receipts and expenditures, a ticketing official, a warehouse official to supervise storage, a communications official to transmit postal news, and an official to ensure proper maintenance of the track. The grade and size of the station will determine the numbers and functions of subordinate officials. A small station can have one official combining several tasks, while in a larger station officials might have two deputies. On a moving train the speed is controlled by the driver, inspection of passengers' tickets is the responsibility of the conductor, the handling of baggage is carried out by the freight official, and the ensurance of safety is the responsibility of the railway guard.

In addition to the individual stations there should be a main station in which would be located a head office responsible for general affairs and the supervision of all subordinate officials. At the same time a board should be set up to make the final decisions on important matters and oversee the head office. Subsequently the head office would appoint a secretary to transmit orders, a personnel officer to direct employees, a treasurer to manage incoming receipts, a cashier to disburse expenditures, an accountant to check the books, a track manager to oversee maintenance and an engineer to inspect the trains. Other posts would be the same as for the individual stations. All potential employees must be examined and, once employed, must submit to regular assessment. After two or three years service railway employees would be eligible for promotion, while after twenty-five years service employees would be entitled to a retirement pension. All those in charge of finance should provide tallies for expenditures and receipts for income; if the authority to spend and receive income is not in the hands of one official then financial control is not properly centralized. All accountants should prepare monthly and yearly reports, and the drawing up of overall figures for income and expenditures should be the responsibility of one person. In this way surpluses and deficits will be clearly seen. This is what is known as balancing expenditures and income and achieving success through efficient office work.

Fares and freight charges depend on the distance. Furthermore, prices might vary according to train speed or be calculated according to a standard uniform rate mutually agreed upon with other companies. The fare regulations drawn up by companies in foreign countries are submitted to their Ministries of Industry and Commerce, which then enforce them. The two ministries lay down tariffs based on construction costs, the amount of passenger and freight traffic, and level of outlays. A national tax is added. Thus we might say that on average a first class passenger would pay 20 copper cash per mile, a second class passenger 15 copper cash and a third class passenger 11 copper cash, with everyone paying an additional two copper cash per mile in tax. Babies would not be charged, young children would pay half-price and soldiers one-quarter price. Freight per ton would be charged 100 copper cash per mile, with an additional six copper cash in tax. If the weight was more than two or three piculs but not yet a ton, then the charge would be the same as for a ton. There are separate tariff rates established for horses, cattle, dogs and sheep, as well as for gold and silver items. During the sixth year of Emperor Guangxu's reign (1880) trains in England carried up to 450 million passengers, while the tonnage of goods moved by train amounted to three-quarters that number. Other countries have more or less have enjoyed similar figures depending on the extent of their railway networks.

These are the broad guidelines involved in the management of railways. It goes without saying that the railroad enhances national revenue and improves the people's livelihood.

Since the beginning of the railroad age in foreign countries construction has experienced myriad changes and expenditures have mushroomed. All possible avenues are pursued in order to encourage interest, whether railroads are built by the state, managed by merchants or even subsidized by government to guarantee private profit. People are very much the same in their love of ease and aversion to work; because of this we must urgently and unremittingly strive to achieve our goal. From the start of our military self-strengthening[12] manufacturing plants have spread in the metropolitan area and in the provinces, and the manufacture of armaments and weapons has gradually adopted Western methods. Yet one of the most crucial factors in the emergence of Western wealth and strength– the building of railroads– has not been considered in our country; such indifference is mainly because people think China has too many natural obstacles, thereby making train travel difficult. However, I think that railroad construction *can* be carried out in China and, furthermore, that it *should* be carried out without delay. Why is this?

There are three reasons: firstly, if we look back to the beginning of railroad construction when all kinds of teething problems arose, noone could have envisaged the scale of changes and improvements required before railroads attained their present satisfactory state. By making use of the previous labour of others it will be easy for us to build railroads now. Secondly, since China has extensive plains linking north and south mountains and rivers can easily be bypassed. Geographical terrain is thus suitable for construction. Thirdly, unlike other countries where everything costs so much and it is expensive to get anything started, China has abundant supplies of timber and iron ore on the one hand and a frugal labour force on the other.

In recent times China's wealth and strength have been exhausted and hardship grows daily. Court and provincial officials during the last few decades have debated over the means to revive prosperity. Yet these debates have been carried out in the dark as if grasping at straws. This is simply because people do not appreciate the potential benefits of alleviating disaster, reducing expenditures and opening up natural resources.[13] What are the reasons for this assertion? If, despite continual reports that a flood or drought is about to usher in disaster, relief from better-off areas is not forthcoming this is due to the problem of inadequate transportation. The problems some areas experience in having an unfavourable man-land ratio because of a burgeoning population or in having too much land because of depopulation caused by epidemics and banditry are due to the difficulty of transferring people from one place to another. In remote areas corrupt officials and criminal elements among the people can often resort to treasonous activities. The fact that higher levels of government do not get to hear of such activities while those at lower levels cannot pass on their reports is due to faulty lines of communication. If, on the other hand, we carried out railroad construction there would be no problems involved in communication and in the movement of goods and people. Hence railroads should be built because they facilitate the alleviation of calamities.

The various means at the state's disposal– such as grain provisions, military supplies and salt levies– all cost money to transport. Such costs exceed the value of the items themselves so that ultimately it is the poorer people everywhere who suffer because of expensive food. This has to do with the problem of inefficient transportation. If, on the other hand, we had railroads there would be yearly savings on the transport costs of purchased grain amounting to millions of *taels*. Hence railroads should be built in the interests of greater economy. It is said that

England attained prosperity because its coal and iron was used by countries all over the world. Today there are Western experts who point out that coal and iron ore deposits in Henan and Shanxi provinces are potentially richer than those in England; however, I have not even heard of coal and iron from Henan and Shanxi being transported more than 1,000 *li* away so how could we expect these resources to be exported overseas in order to compete with English coal and iron! This has to do with an absence of transport. A popular saying goes: 'Beyond a hundred *li* one does not trade in firewood; beyond a thousand *li* one does not trade in grain.' This shows that goods cannot be marketed over long distances. Furthermore, in the name of profit, officials tax whatever trade does exist, assuming that one more customs office will mean the tapping of one more source of revenue. They do not realize that the more burdensome taxes become so people become more impoverished. If the people are more impoverished the country becomes poorer. This is because the relationship between wealth and the country's well-being is akin to that of blood and the body. If blood does not circulate freely the body becomes sick; likewise, if wealth does not circulate freely the country declines. On the other hand the use of railroads will dispel worries concerning unexploited natural resources and stagnant markets. Hence railroads should be built in order to open up resources.

I am not simply presenting a leisurely 'take it or leave it' argument in favour of railroad construction, but rather I am urging that it should be carried out without the slightest delay. If we look at the world beyond China today we see that railroads have appeared in every region bordering our country. England is advancing northwards from India and its railroad has gone beyond Nepal to reach Kashmir. The Russian railroad has gone beyond the Urals, with 200 to 300 *li* of track being built yearly; it has now reached Tashkent and is approaching Khokand. France, with its greedy ambitions to take over Annam, has already explored the sources of several rivers there and is planning to build a railroad directly into Yunnan province. The English again have built a railroad to Burma. The Japanese 'dwarf pirates'[14] are striving to emulate Western ways and, having already joined Tokyo and Kyoto by rail, are now casting their eyes disdainfully across the East China Sea. The Russians have occupied the area around the mouth of the Tumen river and have set up a telegraph office there linking Kyakhta with Moscow. They are also building a railroad to the Amur river in order to facilitate the transport of supplies. If we do not take advantage of the current lull in the international situation and immediately begin the urgent task of building railroads , I fear that within the next few years all the countries surrounding us will have completed construction of their rail networks; then, as soon as relations became less harmonious the foreign powers would be able to profit from the situation and surreptitiously stir up trouble for us. At that point we would be caught unawares, unable to mobilize troops and to set into motion the means of defence. The foreign powers would encroach on our frontier regions in order to control the very heart of China, fragmenting the country and cutting off our grain supplies. Such a scenario is indeed fraught with danger.

Moreover, we should take into account the fact that steamships are now in constant use, enabling Western countries to transport troops to our country in less than forty days; even Russia would be able to transport troops from the Baltic Sea to China in less than fifty days. Could we, on the other hand, move troops from the central provinces to Yunnan or to frontier regions beyond the Great Wall with similar extra-ordinary speed? When one considers that steamships, although slower than trains, can still bring people from tens of thousands of *li* away to our doorstep at such a speed, one can imagine how much quicker it would take in the future when foreign countries have surrounded us with railroads! How would the troops of a relatively well-off province be placed at the disposal of several other provinces, or its wealth be used to finance the armies of other provinces, so that a coordinated system of mutual support might emerge? Only railroads can thwart the foreigners' ambitions to encroach on our border regions and provide adequate defence. This is why I say they should be built without the slightest delay.

Nevertheless, pessimists will still say: ' Even if it is understood that railways can and should be built without the slightest delay, at the end of the day such approval does not tackle the problem of amassing funds. What you have said before on this subject simply pertained to devising regulations for official-merchant joint management, and did not fundamentally broach the question of where the required funds were to come from. Moreover, an imperial edict has already been issued calling for a reorganization of finances and it is clear that each province can hardly save more than a million *taels* while customs revenue does not exceed twenty million *taels*. Yet defence of the eastern coast requires funds, the Western frontier regions are experiencing difficulties in receiving supplies, and there is no more taxable land to mark out. Furthermore, there are never-ending requests from frontier officials pleading poverty and seeking assistance; Board officials in the capital can only look up to the sky in helpless resignation. At such a time is it at all possible to mobilize a huge sum of money? With the national treasury having no reserves, to imagine that one can temporarily rely on the people for such a task is to be unaware of the fact that nine out of ten households have nothing to spare and are as impoverished as the national treasury. Even if there are two or three wealthy people willing to be involved, ultimately it is impossible to achieve anything without support[15] and most people will hesitate to come forward. Moreover, since the law regards the possession of wealth as a trifling matter officials look down on merchants as unimportant. If merchants suffer a mishap they cannot look to officialdom for redress, neither can they seek a legal solution. Who on earth would be willing to court catastrophe by putting one's family and wealth at risk just for the sake of the minutest profit?'

Alas! This response betrays an unawareness of the need to act adroitly according to circumstances. When railroad construction first began there was indeed much uncertainty over the relative merits of official-run or merchant-run enterprises. Today, however, we are beginning to follow in the footsteps of other countries by promoting merchant-run enterprises and this has produced effective results. The government treasury may be empty for the moment, but how could it fail to make use of credit to create a surplus? Also, although the people might be strapped financially how could they collectively fail to amalgamate shares and accumulate large sums of money? Once officials and merchants are of one mind there is nothing that cannot be accomplished.

Yet others might still say: 'If the government carries out this policy of borrowing the foundations of the state[16] will be harmed. If we thoughtlessly encourage a policy of incurring foreign debts our freedom of manoeuvre will be extremely limited.' These people do not understand that all Western countries owe debts worth billions of *taels*, and yet England, France, Germany and Russia are still as powerful as before. As long as we do not borrow at excessive rates of interest and we meet interest repayments on time, why should we fear becoming tied down? Moreover, borrowing money to build railroads is like drawing from one source to replenish another; it is certainly not comparable to borrowing money continuously to pay for indemnities and repaying inherited interest. Moreover, this policy of borrowing money is flexible in another way. The proposed railroads will be solely under merchant management with officials providing cast iron guarantees for the loan. Thus on the surface we will simply be borrowing money, but in reality we will obtain long-term benefits. Foreign capital will be used to improve the Chinese people's standard of living; we will obtain a daily increase of profits with which to repay a yearly diminishing amount of interest.

If people are still unwilling to go along with this policy, having been influenced by the views of mediocrities and hoodwinked by groundless rhetoric, they obviously do not realize that in 1842 (the 22nd year of Emperor Daoguang's reign) China had to pay Britain an indemnity of six million dollars for confiscated opium, as well as three million dollars to compensate British merchants and thirteen million dollars to compensate for Britain's military expenses.[17] Also, in 1860 (the 10th year of Emperor Xianfeng's reign) China had to pay Britain and France four million *taels* and two million *taels* respectively for their expenses in occupying Guangzhou; on top of this China also paid out sixteen million *taels* to cover those two countries' military expenses.[18] Are these sums larger than those required for railroad construction? Just as there was no alternative then, so there is no alternative now to building railroads. If we do not consider building railroads immediately as very important then I fear that in the future we will be compelled to pay out indemnities totalling much more than those already paid. Have you ever thought seriously about the consequences of such a negative attitude?

NOTES

1   Reprinted in *Yangwu yundong*, vol.1, pp.411-418.

2   Emperor Guangxu (r.1875-1908). The nephew of Empress-Dowager Cixi, he was only three years old when he succeeded to the throne and Cixi continued to act as regent. Although Guangxu formally began his personal rule in 1889 Cixi still retained considerable political influence. Guangxu's ill-fated attempt to assert his authority in 1898 by supporting the reform movement resulted in a palace coup and the return to power of Cixi. Guangxu was placed under virtual house arrest for the remainder of his reign.

3   Ma uses a transliteration, *moli*.

4   The province of Ngari (mNga'-ris) was one of the four main regions of Tibet. J.Fletcher, 'Ch'ing Central Asia c.1800', in D.Twitchett and J.Fairbank (eds), *Cambridge History of China*, vol.10 (Cambridge, 1978), p.95.

5   *li*, a unit of length equivalent to .6464 kms or .40057 miles.

6   *tael*: a unit of account equivalent to one Chinese ounce (*liang*) of monetary silver. Ideally, 1,000 copper cash (*qian*) could be used to satisfy a debt of one *tael*. F.King, *Money and Monetary Policy in China 1845-1895* (Cambridge, Mass., 1965), pp.27-28.

7   *zhang*: a unit of length (3.33 metres).

8   *chi*: unit of length, equivalent to 14.1 inches or 35.81 cms.

9   *cun*: unit of length, equivalent to 1/3 decimetre.

10 Ma explains that a French *chi* is equivalent to one Chinese *chi* and eight *cun*.

11 *dan*: unit of dry measure for grain, equivalent to 1 hectolitre.

12 The term used is *junxing* (lit: 'the revival of the military').

13 Ma uses the term *kaiyuan*, which was to figure so prominently in reformist thought at this time.

14 *wokou* (dwarf pirates). This term was a traditional derogatory reference to the Japanese. It is interesting that even a cosmopolitan scholar such as Ma would continue to use it.

15 The term is *guzhang nanming* (lit: 'it is impossible to clap with one hand').

16 Ma uses the term *guoti*. As with his constant reference to *Zhongguo* (China), as opposed to *tianxia* (lit: 'all under heaven', the traditional term describing the Chinese cultural world), Ma demonstrates his move away from a sinocentric world view to one that sees China as a nation state, which is identified with land and people rather than the ruling dynasty. It has also been pointed out that Li Hongzhang used the word *Zhongguo* in a similar way. Kwang-ching Liu, 'The Confucian as Patriot and Pragmatist', in S.Chu and Kwang-ching Liu (eds), *Li Hung-chang and China's Early Modemization*, p.25.

17 According to the Treaty of Nanjing (August 1842), which ended the Opium War, China had to pay an indemnity of $21 million ($12 million for military expenses, $6 million to compensate for the opium destroyed by Chinese officials, and $3 million for the repayment of Chinese merchants' debts to British traders). I.Hsu, *The Rise of Modern China*, p.190.

18 Ma is referring to the Anglo-French military expedition to China in what is known as the Arrow War of 1856. Canton was occupied by Anglo-French forces in 1857, after which they set up a commission to govern the city until a final treaty settlement was reached in 1860.

On the Use of Loans to Build Railroads (1879)[1]

Borrowing is the means whereby the economy is regulated and needs are supplied, and is just as important as trade. Originally people borrowed amongst themselves and governments did not seek to borrow from the people. The idea of a national debt probably originated in ancient Greece during the time of the Persian invasion (corresponding with the Zhou dynasty).[2] At this time there were no funds to pay the troops and so the people had to be solicited for help. The Roman Empire continued with this practice and the state often called on wealthy people to lend it funds. However, the state never won the people's trust, with the result that the people only donated money grudgingly.

Over one thousand years later when countries such as England, France and Austria went to war, military expenditures were enormous. Yet because their rulers were able to obtain the people's trust people willingly loaned money to the government. Thus by the 55th year of Emperor Kangxi's reign (1716) the national debt of these countries totalled more than 7,500 million francs. After another seventy-odd years this total had increased to 12,640 million francs; another twenty years later it had grown to 38,250 million francs. At this time governments just borrowed from their own people; a situation in which countries borrowed from one another or governments sought loans from people in other countries had not yet arisen. After the reigns of Emperor Qianlong and Emperor Jiaqing[3] such practices became widespread. In the 27th year of Emperor Daoguang's reign (1847) the national debt of all these countries had accumulated to 43,276 million francs. At this time money was borrowed simply to pay for military expenditures and provisions rather than to invest in manufacturing industry.

However, during the reigns of Emperor Xianfeng[4] and Emperor Tongzhi[5] the countries of Europe and America experienced a dramatic boom in railroad construction, manufacturing industry and telegraphic communications. Since such activities necessitated huge expenditures governments began to borrow money solely for these purposes. Thereupon in the 9th year of Emperor Tongzhi's reign (1870) the debts of these countries amounted to 97,774 million francs. In the last ten years there have been even more changes and the national debt of foreign countries totals more than two billion francs. India has a debt of 2,575 million francs, Japan and Hong Kong have debts of 43 million francs, Australia has a debt of 894 million francs, and Africa a debt of 991 million francs; the rest is owed by countries in Europe and America.

Now Western countries are not large in area, nor are they especially overpopulated. Yet when it comes to official requests for loans there are more than enough people willing to lend and more than enough funds available to use. It seems that these countries can draw on a source as vast and copious as a wellspring or a river. By what means do they bring about such a situation? They ensure firstly that they gain the people's trust, secondly that they have a clear method of borrowing, and thirdly that they repay loans within a fixed time period. These are the three immutable principles of borrowing, although implementation will differ depending on who is involved.

Westerners say: 'Borrowing money today and paying interest on it later is known as incurring a debt; relying on paying future interest to borrow money is known as having credibility'. Therefore all potential borrowers must have some collateral.

Wealthy merchants rely on their savings, the landed classes rely on their estates and property, and the state relies on its tax revenues. State ministers thus take into account the situation of the state's finances when assessing the possibility of borrowing money. England is normally thought of as a wealthy country; its rate of borrowing is usually at an annual rate of 3%, although in rare cases it has gone up to 4%. The same applies to France. However, with the outbreak of wars the need for military supplies has become more urgent. Consequently England and France had no alternative but to increase the yearly rate of interest to 5 or 6%. Since government ministers were unwilling to be known as incurrers of such a heavy debt, they simply built the increased interest into the original loan. Thus in England loans were discounted from 17 to 21% although the yearly interest rate was set at 3%. In France loans were discounted at 8 to 24%, although the yearly interest rate was 5 or 6%. In Italy, due to insufficient funds, loans are discounted at 51% while the yearly interest rate is 3%. Spain borrowed 300 million francs, discounting it at 58% while the yearly interest rate was 3%. Thus official rates of interest may have been 3% in name, but in fact they were over 6%. Since such loans were for military expenditures and no specific fund was earmarked from which to repay interest, potential creditors were not enthusiastic. They therefore hoarded their money to await an increase in interest.

Now, when it comes to borrowing for the purposes of laying down roads, expanding cultivable land, dredging harbours and building railroads— all of which are activities to improve the people's livelihood (that is to say they are the means by which the sources of wealth can be tapped on behalf of the country)— such a situation is very different from borrowing for military purposes. In the former case everyone jostles for the chance to lend money and swarms of people respond to the opportunity of their own volition, knowing full well they will be repaid with interest. The government of England yearly borrows between 150 million and 175 million francs for public welfare contingencies, while Portugal and India have borrowed up to 30 million francs and Australia 1,100 million francs for the purpose of constructing railroads. France, Austria and Italy borrow thousands of millions to upgrade their railroads. Even a weak and small country like Peru has borrowed 32 million pounds from European countries to build railroads, while a poor country like Tunisia has also borrowed up to 100,000 pounds. The same can be said of countries like Turkey and Egypt.

Thus the way to obtain trust lies in having the means to repay a loan, and the way to repay a loan lies in earmarking funds for repayment. Without such earmarking of funds trust will be skin-deep and potential sources of loan funds will not be very extensive. Simply assuming that if a country is prosperous borrowing will be easy and that if a country is poor borrowing will be difficult is still to be ignorant of the fact that there is a definite basis to obtaining trust.

The ways of seeking a loan are too numerous to detail.[6] If requests for loans are dispersed among the people there is the problem of bringing together dispersed capital; if borrowing is solely sought from the wealthy there is a worry that too much will be asked for. Two hundred years ago Western countries often borrowed from the banks. The big disadvantage of this, however, is that whenever governments were in financial difficulties they had no choice but to yield to the banks in the immediate term; this was not a particularly adept way of seeking loans. A better way was to make sure that the banks and the wealthy were won over through frequent and amicable contact. In this way governments could manage whatever the situation. Otherwise, with few exceptions, governments ran the risk of being muzzled by the banks. In the first year of Emperor Jiaqing's reign loans began to be sought from amongst the people. England began the practice and within ten years 18 million pounds had been obtained. Holland followed and in the 22nd year of Emperor Daoguang's reign[7] obtained over 30 million francs. Austria obtained over 600 million francs in the first year of Emperor Tongzhi's reign. France followed on these countries' heels; although it needed only 3,000 million francs to pay the indemnity to Prussia,[8] as soon as the appeal was launched the subsequent response brought in over 37,000 million francs. Numerous other and weaker countries such as

Russia, Italy and Spain all raised public loans in England and France. The general rate of interest was 5 or 6%, slightly lower than that offered by the banks.

However, fearing people might have misgivings and that it might be difficult to bring together money in one go, governments in the first instance borrowed from the banks, which in turn raised public loans. Yet because the banks were involved and would want to have a share of the spoils, the interest rates might be high. In England, therefore, a way was devised to guard aginst this possibility whereby the government gave advance notice to the banks clearly delineating the amount sought and its preferred rate of interest. The banks willing to make loans then had to send out notices detailing the amount of interest they would charge; the government could then choose from amongst those banks offering the lowest rates. Variously using these borrowing methods countries were able to arrange loans from government and private banks in England and France to finance their industrialization programmes. Several billions were raised and as long as the rate of interest did not exceed 6 or 7% it could be said that this was a successful way of seeking a loan.

With credibility firmly established and the appropriate borrowing strategy arrived at, it would seem no more difficulties should arise. Such an assumption does not take into account the difficulties of repayment. When first seeking a loan arrangements should be made for future repayment. Sometimes double the interest rate is offered to entice creditors; as long as they are living they will receive these interest payments, but if a creditor dies nothing is paid out and the interest is added to that received by other creditors. In this way creditors can receive more interest over a shorter period of time. People are quite happy to go along with this because they always assume they will live long to enjoy the interest and do not imagine they might die and lose all their capital. France still owes this kind of debt to the tune of 7,610,000 francs. In the past this practice was widespread in Europe, but since the advent of life insurance companies it has gradually died out. In addition to repayment of interest a supplementary amount of capital can also be repaid in order gradually to accelerate the repayment of the loan. Depending on how much these extra repayments are, a time limit of between 30 and 90 years is prescribed in which the entire loan is repaid. England, in the 8th year of Emperor Tongzhi's reign, still owes this kind of debt to the tune of £4 million.

Apart from regular interest payments an extra amount might be repaid by means of a lottery draw.[9] Thus while regular interest rates might range from 3.5 to 4%, extra repayments could range from 0.5 to 2%. The regular interest is paid yearly and the additional interest is paid every two years in the form of credit bonds drawn by lottery; those who win can exchange them for cash. Providing generous extra repayments encourages potential borrowers. This method has been used by municipal governments in the West to repair roads, open mines and lay railway tracks; also the building of railroads in Turkey and Egypt has been accomplished especially by this method of borrowing. Furthermore, these bond certificates are inscribed with numbers rather than the recipient's name so as to facilitate circulation. For example, wealthy shareholders of big companies can set aside funds annually to redeem company securities, a process of self-liquidation rather then repayment. Therefore, no matter how a loan is repaid provision is always made to add something extra to the interest. There is no fixed way to deal with emergencies; everything depends on the people involved. How could there be any worries that loans would not be repaid on the one hand, or that repayments might never end on the other?

Now that we are currently discussing the building of railroads our first priority is to raise money. Yet we cannot rely on officials because the government is in straitened financial circumstances, having exhausted its reserves. Neither can we look to the people because they are not accustomed to modern commercial thinking and it would be difficult to attract share capital. There is no other alternative but to borrow from foreign countries. Such a loan would be for the constructive purpose of building railroads, but if we do not in some way make use of Western methods in the arrangements and deal with things appropriately we will not be able to reap the advantages and avoid the pitfalls. I have made some calculations based on my personal experiences. If China really were to incur a foreign debt there are several ways of going about it. There are certain things we should not do, those we should and those we might or might not do depending on who is involved.

The greatest threat to economic well-being is the reaping of unfair gains. There may be a multitude of foreign fims in the treaty ports but there are no more than three or four banks that deal in loans. Furthermore, they are merely overseas branches of foreign banks and their potential loan capital is only sufficient to meet the needs of everyday trade rather than to finance a huge undertaking. In such a situation they would have to seek help from neighbouring banks, which are bound to reap unfair profits. Moreover, we cannot be sure that these three or four banks would not collude with each other and monopolize the money market. Thus even if large banks abroad sent representatives to China it would be difficult for them to escape the control of the treaty port banks. Taking into account our current needs, the only thing for us to do is to take matters into our own hands and discuss arrangements face to face with official and private banks in the capitals of England and France. By so doing we can decide on the cost and interest of the loan ourselves and in one stroke thereby avoid the disadvantage of having to depend solely on the monopolistic control of intermediaries. A proverb notes: 'Those who strive for fame are involved in government, while those who strive for profit are involved in the marketplace'. The capital cities of England and France are the world's most important loan markets. Furthermore, the money borrowed would only be used to purchase rolling stock, machinery, and tracks abroad. If money was raised from within China and remitted abroad in exchange for sterling we would be bound to lose money on the conversion. This would not be as beneficial as using foreign currency borrowed directly from abroad to purchase foreign materials, thereby avoiding the losses accruing from currency exchange as well as monopolistic control by intermediaries. If we do not do this, but rather try to make arrangements within China's various treaty ports it will be difficult to accomplish our aim. This is one of the approaches we should not adopt.

There is a difference between lending money and investing in shares. Investing in shares means taking a yearly bonus from the profits, whereas a creditor only expects to receive a prearranged rate of interest per year. How could we at this time allow foreign merchants to invest in the building of China's railroads deep in the heart of the interior, providing them with the opportunity of interfering in our affairs? Previously, when Turkey embarked on the buiding of railroads shares were mostly held by wealthy English, French and Austrian investors. When Egypt embarked on the construction of the Suez Canal shares were mostly held by French investors; after the Canal was completed it was the French investors who monopolized the profits. A few years ago half of these shares fell into the hands of English investors; subsequently a treaty was signed between England and Egypt allowing all countries to use the Canal and denying Egypt the authority to close the Canal in the event of war. Can we not say that the Canal, far from benefiting Egypt, had in fact brought it many problems? In the past the Frenchman who supervised the building of the Suez Canal, De Lesseps, also proposed to build the Panama Canal in central America, linking the Atlantic and Pacific Oceans. The United States blocked this proposal precisely because of the negative example of the Suez Canal. This is why we cannot invite foreign investment in the building of our railroads and is the other approach we should not adopt.

A considerable period of time is needed to build a railway network, and it cannot be completed in one or two years. Yet during these first two years annual interest on the loan will have to be paid. We cannot make use of the state coffers because reserves are already exhausted and we cannot make use of railroad revenues because the network would not have been completed.The only solution is to adopt the Western method and build into the loan five or six years worth of interest when it is contracted. In this way we will avoid the future danger of transferring funds earmarked for interest payments to other uses, which will damage our credit rating. This is something we must do.

On the Use of Loans to Build Railroads (1879)

The amount of funds needed to build a railway network will come to hundreds of millions of *taels*. We cannot put off indefinitely paying back what we have borrowed, but at the same time we cannot pay it off in one go. Even if we decide to pay back the loan in installments this will still amount to millions of *taels* each time, a sum that is beyond our capabilities to pay. The only solution is to adopt the Western method and add 1 or 1.5 % to the yearly interest payments. By so doing, after about fifty years the debt will be repaid. This is another thing we must do.

China's first railroad should run between Beijing and the Huai River region[10] to facilitate transport and communications. After it has been built profits will increase enormously. However, contracting a foreign debt will mean hundreds of thousands of *taels* in interest being paid out each year. China's railroads will thus become a source of profit for foreigners rather than for us. The only solution is to adopt the Western method of systematically marking government bonds with numbers rather than names, so that once the railroad is making a profit these bonds can gradually be redeemed. This is the third thing we must do.

Contracting a loan is tortuous and difficult business. Sufficient funds can be borrowed on schedule from a bank, whereas it might be difficult to receive all the required funds if you borrow from the public at large. Moreover, banks are keen to make big profits whereas ordinary folk are not so much concerned with making huge profits. Thus if we seek a loan from abroad to build our railroads the wealthy will appreciate the potential and will hanker after the opportunity to invest, while ordinary folk will probably not be aware of potential profit and will have no desire to contribute. It is up to those in charge of contracting the loan to deploy all means in communicating with everyone abroad that this undertaking is for China's benefit. Confidence will thereupon be solid and people will all rush to contribute. The loan will consequently be financed by thousands of small investors and will not be monopolized by the wealthy. Whether one borrows from banks or not, therefore, cannot be decided upon in advance.

The numbers of foreign steel manufacturers cannot be counted on one hand, but the principal ones like Krupps in Germany, Creusot in France and those based in Sheffield (England) each employ 6–7,000 workers and enjoy yearly sales totalling several millions. The owners of foreign steel companies have for a long time yearned for the opportunity to become involved in the profitable business of building railroads in China. If we buy directly from them on credit and acquire the needed rolling stock, machinery and tracks, promising to repay them on a yearly basis once construction has been completed they will be happy to go along with this. This seems a good way to reduce the loan amount and avoid any extra costs due to currency exchange. The only thing to worry about is the possibility that they will arbitrarily increase prices or that they might harbour ambitions of monopolizing supply; in such cases it might be more convenient simply to arrange a straightforward loan. It is up to those in charge of contracting the loan to act as they see fit according to the circumstances and consequently decide on the appropriate plan. Thus whether one buys on credit from the steel manufacturers or not cannot be decided upon in advance. As for raising the money to repay the loan, interest can be built into the loan and repaid in installments or lottery certificates can be sold. One should always be prudent at the beginning since it is difficult to predict whether one false step might lead to even greater mistakes. What one does in these matters will depend on the people involved.

Some might say: 'There must be credibility when contracting a loan, and for credibility to be gained there must be funds earmarked for repayment. In looking towards the foreigners for a loan now where is the credibility going to come from and what is the collateral going to be? Westerners know that China has paid directly for armaments acquired and that funds were borrowed at interest to provide supplies for the north-western campaign.[11] Such transactions were the responsibility of officialdom and funds were clearly earmarked for repayment. Yet today, without firm backing, can we suddenly borrow this huge sum of money we need? Perhaps we might think of designating customs revenue as collateral out of fear that

Westerners will not trust us; yet such a solution does not take into account that customs revenues have already been allocated for other purposes and cannot easily be diverted. In the past when negotiations for a foreign loan were set in motion there were those who raised all kinds of objections and the Board of Revenue subsequently memorialized to have the negotiations stopped. It appears that the idea has not again been raised because it would cause too much trouble'.

I would reply that such an attitude betrays an ignorance of the actual principles involved in borrowing money to build railroads. The railroads that have been built to date in Europe and America cover at least 40,000 miles. Not one country has *not* borrowed funds to complete construction and no country was asked for guarantees. What was relied upon was credibility and the basis for such credibility was simply a detailed inventory drawn up by renowned engineers carrying out surveys on the spot, which outlined the extent of the work to be carried out and the profits to be gained from speedier delivery of goods and people. The main aim of China's railroad network will be to link up north and south. Everyone knows that the profits to be gained from such a network are bound to be the most abundant of all enterprises throughout the country. If we employ an experienced engineer to make a detailed estimate of costs and profits and show this to foreigners credibility will certainly be gained. Why should the government have to earmark customs revenue as collateral before a loan is negotiated?

If there are worries that the benefits from such a huge undertaking will be a long time coming to meet our needs, there is a simple solution. What is this solution? I propose that we first build a line between Tianjin and Beijing to serve as a model. There are six advantages to be gained by first building such a line.

Firstly, although no overall investigation has been carried out in China I have heard that an English engineer has already carried out a survey between Tianjin and Beijing. We can make use of his survey in carrying out further investigations, thereby obtaining twice the benefit for half the work put in. Secondly, the distance between Tianjin and Beijing is no more than 200 *li*.

We could therefore expect to complete the line within a year and thus the benefits will quickly be apparent. Thirdly, a line linking north and south will take more than one or two years to complete. The initiation of such a colossal project will inevitably raise anxiety and doubt. Once a line between Tianjin and Beijing is completed steamship traffic from the south can then be transferred to trains on reaching Tianjin. Everyone, including scholars, ordinary folk, officials and merchants, will then find such a line extremely convenient. When the time comes to build a north-south line there will be no problem in attracting investment funds, and communications will be speeded up. Fourthly, building railroads and telegraphs in China will be a pioneering endeavour and the ignorant will inevitably rise up to condemn the idea, insisting that although such projects may be appropriate in foreign countries they are not so in China. If a line is built between Tianjin and Beijing people will clearly perceive the convenience of speedy travel between the two points and everyone will eventually regard the railroad as a familiar part of the landscape. Moreover, those who usually rely on transportation for their livelihood will be able to work for the railroad loading and unloading goods and transferring luggage. Compared to the past, therefore, railroads can only bring benefit and not harm. People will thus come to appreciate that building railroads is meant to benefit both the country and the people. They will view railroads only in terms of the advantages gained from easier commercial intercourse and certainly not as a harmful threat to their livelihoods. Those petty Confucian scholars who might one day dabble in Western learning will not click their tongues in disapproval and *qingyi*[12] advocates will not high-handedly raise their voices in criticism. It will be seen that such a line represents the beginning of a change in our fortunes.

Fifthly, the difficulties railroads might present do not lie with the actual construction but in incompetent management. To build a north-south line requires thousands of workers and several hundred supervisors. Since we Chinese have no experience of railroad construction we would be forced to hire foreigners and this would mean innumerable extra costs.

But if we first build a line between Tianjin and Beijing we can make use of the opportunity to select some of our own people to learn management skills, how to lay railroad tracks, how to drive engines, and how to attend to accounts. In the future their experience can be used in the construction of a north-south line.

Finally, if we suddenly begin to construct a railway network creditors will not have much confidence and the interest demanded on any loan will probably be high. An immense number of books on China written by Westerners all put forward the idea that because political power is dispersed officials can line their own pockets. If our railroads were to be supervised and managed by officials, although foreign creditors might consider this a guarantee for profit they might also fear that authority over the enterprise will become fragmented. Official embezzlement might set in, leading to long term corruption of the system and subsequent losses for creditors. They will thereupon increase interest on the loan as a last ditch attempt to retrieve the situation, or send their own trusted appointees as supervisors to check up on everything. Today, if we build a Tianjin-Beijing line we will be able to use the appropriately qualified people and ensure that the system is in good working order. If we are prudent at the beginning we will gradually establish the foundation for the system's expansion in the future; foreign creditors will supply all the funds, confident that no cheating or deception will occur. Also, even if at the beginning interest rates are high the amount of funds needed for the Tianjin-Beijing line will not be great and so our interest repayments will not be excessive. Later, when foreigners see how successful the railroad is they are bound to reduce the interest on the larger loans we will have to contract for further construction. The building of a Tianjin-Beijing line will thus in the long term give us credibility.

Since widespread communications are the basis of gaining wealth, borrowing funds is a contingency measure. Although this is a stopgap measure it is the means whereby our fortunes will be improved and will be a symbol of our country's revival. Furthermore, we need to ensure that the arrangements for the loan take into account all possible problems. If instead we worry about what could go wrong and reject the idea of a loan altogether, would not this be the same as worrying about sexual indulgence and therefore banning marriage, or worrying about a shortage of wild animals and therefore proscribing the hunt? Surely, we dare not imagine this!

On the Use of Loans to Build Railroads (1879)

NOTES

1 Reprinted in *Yangwu yundong*, vol.1, pp.418-425.

2 Zhou dynasty (1122 B.C-256 B.C.).

3 Emperor Qianlong (r.1736-1795), the 4th emperor of the Qing dynasty; Emperor Jiaqing (r.1795-1821), the 5th emperor of the Qing dynasty.

4 Emperor Xianfeng (r.1850-1861), the 7th emperor of the Qing dynasty.

5 Emperor Tongzhi (r.1861-1875), the 8th emperor of the Qing dynasty.

6 *nan geng pu shu* (lit: 'it would be difficult to enumerate the numbers of attendants who would have to be changed'). Ma is alluding to a passage from the *Li Ji* (Book of Rites), in which the Duke of Lu asks Confucius to explain the proper conduct of the scholar. Confucius replies: 'If I were to enumerate the points in it summarily I could not touch upon them all; if I were to go into details on each, it would take a long time. You would have changed all your attendants-in-waiting before I had concluded'. J.Legge, *The Li Ki, Part iv (Oxford, 1885), p.402.*

7 Emperor Daoguang (r.1821-1850), the 6th emperor of the Qing dynasty.

8 Ma is referring to the aftermath of the Franco-Prussian War (1870-1871).

9 In 1869 the American missionary, Young J.Allen, had suggested that the Chinese government could raise money by selling national bonds (*guozhu*) to the wealthy. A.Bennett, *Missionary Journalist in China* (Athens, Georgia, 1983), pp.133-135.

10 The Huai River region in central China encompasses the provinces of Anhui and Jiangsu.

11 Ma is referring to the military campaigns waged by the dynasty against Moslem rebellions in Shaanxi, Gansu and Xinjiang, which broke out in 1862. Those in Shaanxi and Gansu were crushed in 1873, although the rebellion in Xinjiang lingered on until 1877.

12 *qingyi* (lit: 'pure talk') was a reference to the memorials submitted by a group of officials and scholars in the 1870s and 1880s insisting that China adopt a policy of uncompromising resistance against foreign encroachment. They also condemned the adoption of Westernizing measures as a betrayal of traditional Confucian values.

On Enriching the People (1890)[1]

Wealth and strength are together the foundations on which a state is governed, but the prerequisite of strength is the attainment of prosperity. If we look back to the period between the reigns of the Kangxi and Qianlong emperors[2] it is clear that expenditures were met although taxes were not always levied and that domestic markets were sufficient even though overseas trade was banned.[3] However, since the military crisis and the opening up of China to foreign trade, the revenue from customs receipts and *lijin* taxes yearly gross over 20 million *taels* while merchant trade yearly amounts to 200 million *taels*. Yet the state coffers are running low and very few villages have been able to store supplies. Why is the situation so different from what it was one hundred years ago? In the past indigenous products were traded within the country by the Chinese people themselves in order to circulate money within China. That is to say, the government's needs could be supplied from within the country. It was just like 'taking goods from the central treasure-house and concealing them in the outer store';[4] wealth was constantly circulated without being dispersed outside the country.

Today it is not so. Since the emergence of Sino-foreign trade the amount of goods foreigners exchange for our silver has increased yearly while the amount of goods *we* exchange for *their* silver has yearly diminished. At the same time the need for Beijing and the provinces to purchase an ever increasing number of cannons and steamships becomes more urgent. Thus the yearly surplus of imports over exports is never less than 30 million *taels*. Over the last thirty years our trade deficit must have totalled millions and millions of *taels*! Our own natural resources have not yet been exploited and our mines have long been closed. With a situation such as this it is no wonder that our silver specie is exhausted and the people are poor.

China, however, is not the only country involved in foreign trade. From the time Korea signed treaties[5] there is not one country amongst the five continents that closes its ports and rejects diplomatic relations with others. Britain, the United States, France, Russia, Germany and British India all attain wealth through trade. Having resided in some of these countries and explored the origins of their prosperity it is clear to me that all countries consider foreign trade as a necessary principle of life. If a country trades and its exports exceed its imports, this is profitable; if a country's exports and imports are balanced, this is also profitable; but if a country's imports exceed its exports, this is of no benefit. When Britain and the United States could not profit from foreign trade they exploited their own natural resources by opening up mines, thereby making up for their trading deficits. When their natural resources became insufficient these countries did not hesitate in crossing the oceans to knock on our doors, signing treaties to obtain compensation from us.

With the situation being like this, the grand strategy for achieving wealth is clearly discernible. If we desire China's prosperity then there is no alternative other than to increase our exports while reducing our imports. If our exports increase then wealth that has already been drained can be accumulated again. If our imports are reduced then wealth that has not yet been drained will not again be so. Given the case, however, that some wealth already drained is not easy to accumulate, surely it is better to exploit our own mineral resources. If we take this initiative the money spent on labour will not leave the country and we will be responsible for the accumulation of our own natural wealth without relying on foreign assistance. In so doing we will be able to balance our imports and exports. I propose the following measures.

To enhance the volume of our exports we need to improve considerably the quality of our well established products in order to expand their markets. China's two principal products are silk and tea. When we first started to trade with the West our silk and tea exports were sufficient to balance imports of foreign opium and cloth. In recent years, however, silk and tea production in British India has flourished, impinging on our profits. If we look at India just over ten years ago, its silk exports were only worth one million *taels* and its tea exports only five million *taels*. Last year India's silk exports were already worth over 2,700,000 *taels* and its tea exports 16,000,000 *taels*. Recently, Japanese silk and tea production has been greatly flourishing, and each year exports of those products have been worth nearly ten million *taels*. China's yearly silk exports are now worth over 32 million *taels* and the value of tea exports is about the same. Yet in these last ten years or so the increase in Chinese silk and tea exports has not exceeded a few million *taels* and is clearly not as rapid as the yearly increases in Indian and Japanese exports. If we do not adopt timely measures to rectify the situation then in the future production in the other countries will daily grow and their sales will be unlimited, whereas we will stagnate and remain at this year's figure of 60 million *taels* or so; this will continue until they completely take over our markets. There are three ways to improve the situation.

Firstly, we must pay attention to some fundamental aspects of sericulture and tea production. Having personally looked into how sericulture is carried out in France and Italy I discovered that by skilfully planting mulberry trees the leaves grow lush and healthy and that careful breeding ensures plump and sturdy silkworms. Those that become diseased are separated out for treatment and fed separately so as to avoid infection. Just when the chrysalis is on the verge of becoming a moth the cocoon is dried and pressed through baking so that it can be stored even longer. Our experts who write and talk about silkworm cultivation have never heard of this before. In other countries, however, technical schools are established to provide instruction for the people. Thus the reeling of silk can take place over a long period of time and especially lengthy and fine thread is produced. Although foreign sericulture is handicapped by the poor quality of the mulberry trees and the soil, and the silk is not as pliable as Chinese silk, it is in fact more lustrous and uniformally pure than Chinese silk. People are therefore quite happy to buy it.

Again, if we look at the cultivation of tea in India– the methods of planting, investigation of soil conditions, adaptation to the seasons, the picking of leaves when they have sprouted, the trimming of branches, how the leaves are dried under the sun, roasted and then moistened to enhance their colour density (whether using manpower or machines)– every stage of the production process has an organized schedule. Therefore, although the quality of Indian tea is not as good as the Chinese product, its colour, fragrance and taste are all perfectly acceptable; it is pure and fresh and not bitter, leaving a sweet aftertaste on the back of the tongue. It is not surprising that the market for Indian tea has gradually expanded. At this time the court should order the viceroys and governors of those provinces which engage in sericulture and tea cultivation to instruct their subordinates to investigate, and seek knowledge of, Western methods. We should appreciate the advantages of such methods and not hold on obstinately to prejudiced views. In this way the sources of our indigenous wealth will not be replaced by foreign products.

Secondly, merchant capital in the tea and silk trades must be consolidated. The basis of Western commercial superiority lies with the joint stock company. All large undertakings and trade enterprises necessarily involve the accumulation of distributed shares, which facilitates an increase in the amount of capital. If the company suffers a loss then there is enough capital to cushion the effects and the company will not be vulnerable to foreign domination. In China the costs of exporting silk and tea come to about 60 million *taels*, but the trade is dispersed and each merchant runs his own business. Initially, each merchant goes to the local producing area and competes with others as to who will obtain the first purchases. The local producers take advantage of the situation and raise the price, thereby already increasing the costs. Then the merchants compete in an overcrowded market; their original capital not being sufficient, they borrow funds from native banks at a discount. If the tea has to be stored the costs are higher. Finally, the foreign merchants are able to perceive the merchants' predicament and deliberately do not offer a price straightaway. With the deadline approaching to pay back the bank loan and the interest accumulating, merchants have no option but to sell at a reduced price in order to speed up sales. Thereupon everyone competes as to who will sell the quickest, with the result that the previously high price suddenly declines in the blinking of an eye. This is precisely the reason why year after year the losses suffered by the tea and silk trades amount to several millions of taels. Today, if we can really bring together dispersed merchant capital to form several joint stock companies, and elect boards of directors as managers, then the bulk purchase price can be easily negotiated and there would be no worries about a sudden rise in the price. With a substantial amount of capital, a low purchase price and minimal rates of interest, when the goods reach port there will be no need for a rushed sale. Henceforth, foreign merchants would no longer lead us by the nose; we would be able to sell when it suited us and losses would be rare.

Thirdly, we must reduce *lijin* and ordinary duties on tea and silk. When foreign trade with the West first began there were no precedents for duties. An investigation of the maritime customs receipts from Guangzhou reveals that duties were originally set at 5%. Each picul of tea sold for about 50 *taels*; the duty levied on each picul therefore amounted to two and a half *taels*. Today each picul of lesser quality tea sells for 10 *taels* but the same amount of duty is still levied.[6] Apart from duties there is the *lijin* tax. With both duties and *lijin* to pay, which in some cases together nearly amount to the selling price, it is no wonder that the tea trade is in difficulties. Foreigners assist their merchants primarily by increasing duties on imports while reducing those on exports. In China the situation is the reverse.

It would be more appropriate now for us to vary the amount of duty levied on tea according to its quality; the *lijin* tax could then also be reduced progressively. With light duties and reduced *lijin* the selling price would be cheaper, hence facilitating an increase in exports which in turn will generate additional revenue from duties. On a daily basis such revenue might not seem much, but on a monthly basis there will be a surplus. Thus in the beginning there may be little taken in revenue and there will be deficits, but in the long run there is bound to be ample recompense and a surplus. If we look at the effects of customs barriers in recent times it is evident that in general lenient tariffs bring long term benefits, while burdensome tariffs produce only short-term gain; the advantages and disadvantages of both are plain to see.

Moreover, tariffs on trade are not set in stone. As soon as the time arrives when the treaties are revised we can raise the relatively light tariffs on foreign goods according to their value. For example, even though goods such as wine and Philippine tobacco are taxed very heavily in foreign countries— as much as 100%— they are not taxed after entering our treaty ports because they are considered as products solely for the use of foreigners. A revision of the treaties will enable us to tax these products while reducing the duties on our exports, which will be to our benefit. If the Zongli Yamen holds firmly to this strategy foreign countries will fall into line. Thus with the improved quality of tea and silk production, the accumulation of capital, and the reduction of taxes and duties we will in the future be able to compete successfully with Indian and Japanese production. A yearly increase in our exports to the value of several million *taels* will then occur automatically.

Apart from tea and silk, other Chinese products that are continuously exported abroad include leather, sheep's wool, sugarcane, plaited straw items, cotton, porcelain and rhubarb. Appropriate improvements should also be made to their production. All this can be described as enhancing the quality of one's exports in order to retrieve wealth that has already leaked out of the country.

The second measure concerns the reduction of foreign

imports by manufacturing the same kinds of goods that are currently being imported so as to compete with foreigners in the marketplace. In addition to opium the principal foreign imports are cotton cloth and cotton yarn.[7] Britain possesses about 150,000 looms, the United States 130,000 and India from twenty to thirty thousand. Each loom produces two bolts of cotton cloth every twenty-four hours. Thus 310,000 looms daily produce 620,000 bolts of cotton cloth. In one year (on the basis of 360 days) it is possible to produce 223,200,000 bolts of cloth. Calculating from the last ten years China has yearly imported about 15 million bolts of foreign cloth worth 30 million *taels*. This represents only 7% of factory production in Britain and the United States. As for imports of foreign yarn, in the last ten years or so they have been worth only several hundred thousands of *taels* yearly. However, because of the fineness and purity of foreign yarn, within the last few years all provinces in the north have competed to purchase it. Last year imports of yarn were worth 13,500,000 *taels*. Production of cotton occurs everywhere in China; in Songjiang and Taicang (in Jiangsu province), for example, yearly production of cotton amounts to no less than five or six million piculs. For our policymakers to abandon indigenous cotton production now and passively allow the people to use foreign cotton for their clothes and quilts is certainly not the way to strive for national prosperity.

In the fifth year of Emperor Guangxu's reign (1879), the Commissioner of Trade for the Northern Ports, Li Hong-zhang,[8] submitted a memorial proposing the creation of a textile plant. More than ten years have passed and scant success has been achieved. The reasons for this are that capital was insufficient and management was probably not as efficient as it should have been. Today there is therefore a need to reorganize. During these last ten years, while no other textile plant was allowed to be established, this sole plant was only equipped with 200 to 300 looms.[9] Only 500-600 bolts of cloth were produced daily, that is to say a yearly total of 180,000 bolts. This constituted a mere one-eightieth of the total amount of foreign imports. Thus in these ten years the proportion of trade taken away from the foreigners has been a mere drop in the ocean.[10] Furthermore, the expenses for the machinery were enormous. With less cloth woven the expenses are even more burdensome, making a dent in the operating capital. If more cloth were produced then expenses would not be so heavy and profits would steadily accumulate.

I propose that either the amount of capital invested in the textile plant be increased or another plant be established; we should then strive to produce a yearly amount of cotton cloth that would be equivalent to one-tenth of foreign imports. Only this policy will allow us to regain our economic rights.[11] I feel sure that with the employment of personnel skilled in administration and management beneficial results will be evident within ten years. Afterwards, we could adopt similar practices in the production of eiderdown, heavy woollen cloth, camlet and blankets. If we ensure that China produces a fraction more goods than before, foreigners accordingly will gain that little less profit; Chinese industry and commerce will thus become that little more prosperous. All this is what I call emulating foreign manufacturing in order to accumulate wealth that has not yet been drained.

Thirdly, if we want to guarantee the ongoing accumulation of wealth without worrying about its occasional dispersal, we need to rely on the potential wealth of mineral resources. We have many kinds of mineral resources, with the most useful being coal and iron ore. However, coal and iron ore provide the means to bring about wealth; they do not represent wealth in themselves. Those that do are gold and silver. As scientists have quite rightly pointed out, the use of steam power began a mere forty-odd years ago. Yet we can see that in the countries of Europe and North America railway tracks extend over 600,000 *li*, hundreds of thousands of steamships travel to and fro, iron chimneys soar to the high heavens, and mines are dug deep into the bowels of the earth.[12] Furthermore, bridges have been built over rivers and lakes, tunnels have been bored into the mountains, land has been reclaimed from the sea and gigantic armaments have been produced. People have utilized the hidden and subtle force of electricity, heat and light, phenomena that have no shape or sound, to achieve these unprecedented technological feats. A concrete analysis of the expenses involved in these endeavours reveals that they amounted to not less than 20,000 million *taels*.

So what really is the explanation for these achievements? Can it be that people are far more talented than those of previous times? If not, how does one explain this outburst of energy? There is no other explanation other than that during the last years of Emperor Daoguang's reign wealth was discovered underground in Melbourne and San Francisco.[13] From the time America was discovered in the middle years of the Ming dynasty[14] to the last years of Emperor Daoguang's reign totals approximately four hundred years. It has been a little over twenty years from the last years of Emperor Daoguang's reign to the tenth year of Emperor Tongzhi's reign (1871). If we calculate the amount of gold and silver mined during this latter period it already totalled an equivalent of 12,000 million *taels*. This figure represents more than twice the amount mined in the previous four hundered year period. Also, since the tenth year of Emperor Tongzhi's reign up to the present more modern, effective and easily used mining machinery has been developed so that the amount of gold and silver extracted has doubled again. Thus during this forty year period (1850–1890) the amount of gold and silver obtained is one hundred times more than during the previous four hundered years. Such countless wealth has facilitated the exploitation of yet more natural resources; talented people are busy everywhere embarked on a never-ending quest to change the face of the old world. Today, China is in the process of building a navy, is striving to establish manufacturing industry, proposes to begin iron mining, and is planning to construct a railway from Beijing to Hankou.[15] Such projects are unprecedented in China's history, but I fear that if we simply rely on the limited amount of money that is currently in circulation to finance them this will be insufficient.

I once heard that a mining engineer, in discussing gold mining, pointed out that a land continent would inevitably contain a spine of mountains extending over tens of thousands of *li* and that valuable mineral deposits would form along such mountain ranges. Thus the Rocky Mountains comprise the spine of North and South America; gold and silver deposits have formed along the range in San Francisco, Mexico and Chile. The continent of Australia has the Blue Mountains as its spine, and their mineral deposits have given rise to mining activity around Melbourne.

The Asian continent has the Kunlun Mountains as its principal artery; it stretches north-westwards to the Urals and south-eastwards through central Tibet to the provinces of Yunnan and Sichuan. All along this chain lay hidden mineral deposits of potentially great value. The northern branch of the Kunlun passes through the Southern and Northern Tianshan, then winds its way through the Altai and Kentei Mountains, skirting the ranges of the Greater and Lesser Khingan mountains to reach Zhangbaishan in the northeast.[16] From Hamyong in Korea the mountain range stretches to Lushun in Fengtian province before extending southwards under the sea (where it appears as a series of jagged islets in shallower waters), eventually forming the Rong,Cheng,Deng and Lai mountain ridges in Shandong province and culminating in Taishan.[17] Gold and silver deposits exist all along this chain. There are never-ending references to the huge numbers of mineworkers in the vicinity of the Southern and Northern Tianshan, which possess the most bountiful gold deposits. Russian miners in the Greater Khingan mountains yearly obtain gold worth several millions of *taels*. The area around the Mo river has just begun to recruit labour and gold mining is flourishing there.[18] In former times there were assembled in the mountains of Jilin province countless thousands of 'gold bandits' making a living from the deposits. In Hamyong and other places in Korea there are more than 70,000 gold miners; after payment of official taxes, the amount of gold mined is yearly worth the equivalent of two to three million *taels*.

I previously visited the mountains of Ninghai and Zhaoyuan[19] and saw for myself the mines that had been sunk in olden times. They stretched for as long as several tens of *li* and were as deep as thirty metres. I could clearly feel with my hands the indentations that had been cut into the cliff edge. Huge amounts must have been spent on such projects. Today the abandoned low quality ores and slag from the mines can be found everywhere in the mountains and on the valley floors. An inspection of these rocks and chippings revealed that they all contained traces of gold. A mining engineer was asked to carry out a survey of the area, and he concluded that rich veins of gold extended in an unbroken chain as long as 60 to 70 *li* deep in the mountains. It was also discovered that every ton of chiselled ore contained fifty grams of gold, an amount visiting Western engineers compare to that extracted from the earliest mines in San Francisco. Thus we have both the evidence of previous mining activity and the testimony of mining experts mutually confirming the potential for gold mining. In Shandong, for example, although its three eastern prefectures jut out into the sea like the handle of the Big Dipper and the width of the peninsula from north to south is no more than 300-400 *li* (therefore covering a small area), its potential mining wealth in the north almost equals that of San Francisco and Melbourne combined. Furthermore, northern Shandong adjoins the Gulf of Bohai, thereby facilitating convenient transportation; transshipment of minerals is also made easy because Shandong is situated midway between north and south. Compared to the Greater Khingan mountains, where people rarely go and freezing temperatures make approach roads impassable, it is far easier to initiate mining projects in northern Shandong.

Another case concerns the Pingdu gold mine.[20] When it began operations working capital was not sufficient and the costs had to be met by continuous loans. Also the mining engineers employed at the start were unable to calculate the depth and length of the vein, how much gold it contained, and how easy it woud be to separate out the gold using sulphuric acid. Nevertheless, the mine directors still went ahead and commissioned them to construct the mine, purchase machinery and sink the shaft. By the time the directors realized that the project might be held up by the engineers the deadline for repaying the loans had arrived and it was not possible to borrow any more . The mine directors were thus in dire financial straits. Outsiders, not knowing the real reason, simply attributed the crisis to the unreliability of gold mining. They did not consider that from the time the mine opened up till now expenditures for the operating machinery totalled more than 200,000 *taels*, for storage 20-30,000 *taels*, for workers' wages more than 100,000 *taels*, for the mining engineers' salaries 50-60,000 *taels*, and for interest payments on loans 40-50,000 *taels*. On the other hand, the more than thirty tons of rock being mined today has a gold content worth over 100,000 *taels*. Supposing all the loans were converted into working capital that did not have to be paid back at a certain time, then if we set the value of the gold currently being extracted against the amounts of money already spent, we cannot say with certainty that the mine is not profitable.

The only really profitable mine in China is the Kaiping coal mine.[21] For the first ten or so years of its existence no interest payments on share dividends were paid out. Although experiencing several losses the mine still survives today in a healthy state. If the mine directors had been ordered to return all the share capital to investors then Kaiping would simply have faced the same financial crisis as Pingdu. If Pingdu had its own operating capital like Kaiping, then even though it might run the same risks experienced by Kaiping in the past, who could say whether in the future Pingdu might be more prosperous than Kaiping is today? If we do not at this time strive to support the Pingdu mine and simply allow it to close down, then we would have failed at the last hurdle.[22] I fear that such a scenario will not only result in the loss of Pingdu but will also make it very difficult for China's mining industry as a whole to be revived. I propose calling on the Commissioner of Trade for the Northern Ports, Li Hongzhang, to make an overall calculation of the costs and then augment the mine's capital so that it can continue to operate. We can then expect that in the future profits will clearly be forthcoming.

I also propose that subsequent to a thorough investigation of the Ninghai and Zhaoyuan mines the rock extracted from the shafts sunk be grounded into powder. Afterwards the powder should be mixed with mercury, filtered and then heated with sulphur to produce smelted gold. Such a process carried out daily will obtain a definite amount of gold from every ton of rock extracted. Armed with a realistic estimate of the profits to be gained over several years and of the amount of capital needed, mining operations could then be set in train. Within a few years I predict that gold and silver will be endlessly pouring forth from the 'mud and sand'. With gold mines leading the way, other mining operations will follow and our sources of profit will become widespread. With the availability of such resources we will gradually be able to build railways linking north and south and revive agriculture in the northern border regions. The United States has only been established for one hundred years, and its inhabitants are all immigrant labourers. Australia has only been opened up during the last one hundred years. Yet in terms of railways crisscrossing the land and the prosperity of agriculture, these two countries rank first in the world. This has been entirely due to the wealth accrued from the exploitation of gold resources. If China decides not to emulate Western methods, then there is no more to be said; if, however, China *does* desire to make use of Western methods in order to seek wealth, then there is no other way but to begin by opening up gold mines. Otherwise the people will remain poor and the national coffers will remain depleted. Simply to wring one's hands and lament the lack of means to achieve wealth is to be ignorant of the fact that Heaven has not abandoned China and that there is indeed gold buried in the mountains just waiting to be exploited. Such a scenario is no different from wealthy grandfathers and fathers storing gold in the cellars of their houses to bequeath to descendants who later on do not know actually how to put it to good use. Would not this be a great pity?

When all is said and done, however, my three grand strategies– improving indigenous products, emulating the production of Western goods, and exploiting valuable mineral resources– all need funds. If we want to accrue wealth we must first spend wealth. It is a universal fact that one cannot reap without first sowing and that one cannot gain profit without first undergoing effort and experiencing difficulty. At the present time government funds are exhausted on the one hand, and on the other the people's livelihood is precarious; neither the country nor the people have the means to implement effectively these three grand strategies. Surely, we cannot accept things as they are, but what can be done to bring about a change? There is no better way than to emulate Western countries and set up a bureau of commercial affairs. Such a bureau would come under the jurisdiction of the navy, but its external affairs would be administered by the Northern and Southern Commissioners of Trade or by chosen individuals experienced in commercial affairs stationed in the major treaty ports working with the Northern and Southern Commissioners.

Afterwards this bureau of commercial affairs would secure a loan from various foreign countries totalling 20-30 million *taels*. Such a loan agreement would be signed by the bureau itself or perhaps by another newly established general trading company exclusively concerned with commercial affairs. The funds would be drawn upon for a period of ten years. A yearly interest of 4-5% together with the original borrowed amount, would begin to be repaid after twenty years; otherwise the interest could be increased to 6.5% (to be repaid yearly) for a period of 50-60 years as the equivalent of paying back capital and interest. With the borrowing arrangements settled the bureau of commercial affairs could then proceed with implementing the important measures relevant to the three strategies mentioned above: the exploitation of gold mines, promotion of machine textile production and improvement of silk and tea production. Such measures should be carried out in an orderly way, beginning with the easiest and moving on to the more difficult.

The way this should be done overall is to encourage merchants to pool shares and set up a joint stock company.[23] With a firm financial base as protection this company could afterwards borrow funds from the bureau of commercial affairs; the yearly interest obtained from such loans could be used to repay the foreign debt. If merchant shareholders themselves find it difficult to move ahead with an important commercial initiative and investment capital is not forthcoming, the bureau of commercial affairs could provide a loan to kick-start the project. The interest charged on loans extended to Chinese merchants should be slightly higher than that paid on the foreign loan. The difference will be sufficient both to enable repayment of the foreign interest and to cover any losses resulting from currency exchange. Funds can therefore always be scooped up from one source or the other.

Critics might say: 'You are seeking to promote commerce because silver is being siphoned out of the country by foreigners. Yet today this very promotion of commerce would result in the yearly repayment of several million taels to service the foreign debt, thereby increasing the drainage of silver out of the country. We would suffer losses before achieving any gain, and the original aim of such a strategy would thus be unfulfilled'. Such people do not realize that if commerce prospers then imports will decrease and exports increase; the former situation, in which Chinese silver left the country, would be reversed and an abundance of foreign silver will flood into China. Furthermore, although we will initially be making use of foreign silver to exploit our gold resources ultimately Chinese gold will be sold for foreign silver. This is just like using the weapons of an opponent for one's own advantage. Also, while a small amount of silver will leave the country in the form of yearly interest payments, in the long run Chinese merchants will still gain profits at the expense of foreigners. How could this possibly be seen as a 'drainage of silver'?

Critics will also say: 'Although foreign merchants establish public companies in their own countries to encourage commerce and to provide mutual loans to the tune of millions, we have never heard of official involvement or guarantees. Since official backing for merchant loans has never occurred in foreign countries, why should China alone attempt to put such an idea into practice?' These people do not understand that in other countries merchants can travel freely across national boundaries and that they are not subject to any restrictions on production and transportation. Furthermore, merchants from one country can join with other merchants in another to set up joint stock companies. Thus in Europe and America wealthy merchants from England are involved in setting up countless numbers of enterprises, while English stockholders are on the directors' boards of railway and telegraph companies as well as of gold and silver mine companies. Likewise, European and American merchants all do business in the English colonies. Consequently, merchants from different countries all manage mutual borrowing themselves; they do not need to get the backing of government officials. Such a situation does not exist in China. This is because foreigners in China cannot engage in manufacturing or the reprocessing of native goods,[24] while Chinese merchants have not as yet been able to set up joint stock companies with foreigners. Since each side disparages the other, Chinese merchants have no other alternative but to rely on their government to secure a loan. If upstanding ministers in whom there is public confidence act as official guarantors and the state's obligations are enshrined in regulations then foreign merchants will all be happy to proceed. In this way a large loan of several millions of taels can immediately be negotiated. If we select those who have a good understanding of commerce to be involved in this endeavour and if they wholeheartedly strive for concrete benefits then there will be no worries that losses might outweigh gains. This being the case, within several years the poor will become wealthy; when the people are prosperous the country itself will be strong. Thus while it may seem in name that officials will be borrowing on behalf of merchants in order to initiate this endeavour, the ultimate benefits that will accrue from such a strategy mean that officials in fact are borrowing on behalf of the entire country. Why then be reluctant to adopt this plan? One aspect of my proposed national loan that should be mentioned is that it provides at the present time the opportunity for ruler and people together to break through the barriers of stagnation; it should not be used for military purposes but rather must be used to promote commerce.

NOTES

1 Reprinted in *Yangwu yundong*, vol.1, pp.403-411.

2 Emperor Kangxi (r.1661-1722), the 2nd emperor of the Qing dynasty.

3 The principle of light taxation (*qingyao bofu*) was an ideal of Confucian government and it was expected that emperors reduce taxes in areas hit by bad harvests or natural calamities. Kangxi, for example, reduced land and grain taxes on numerous occasions between 1662 and 1705. In 1713, in accordance with another principle of 'never raising taxes' (*yong bujia fu*), Kangxi fixed the amount of *ding* tax (originally a labour corvee that had been commuted into a money payment) for adult males; an increase of adult males after 1713 was not subject to further tax. This limit was then applied to the land tax, especially after the two taxes were merged in the late eighteenth century. Henceforth, land tax quotas remained the same, although the rate of collection continued to increase. Wang Yeh-chien, *Land Taxation in Imperial China 1750-1911* (Cambridge, Mass., 1973). Ma's reference to the banning of overseas trade is to the period 1662-1683 when the Qing dynasty closed all ports to foreign trade in response to the coastal raids carried out by Ming loyalists from their stronghold in Taiwan. With the pacification of Taiwan in 1683 the ban on foreign trade was lifted and customs houses were opened in Canton, Zhangzhou and Ningbo. Motivated again by security concerns, the dynasty restricted foreign trade to Canton after 1757.

4 Ma's reference comes from the *Chunqiu* (Spring and Autumn Annals), a chronicle of events from 722-481 B.C and believed to have been compiled and edited by Confucius. A minister of Jin suggests to his lord that valuable horses and jade be presented to the state of Yu in order to allow the army of Jin to pass through on its way to subjugate the state of Guo. In response to the lord's objection that such horses and jade were valuable assets, the minister notes that they are simply being placed in an outer treasury (*waifu*) for the time being (implying that once Jin had conquered Guo it would be in a position to occupy Yu). See J.Legge, *The Chinese Classics, vol.5, part 1* (London, 1872), p.136.

5 Korea signed its first treaty with a Western power (the US) in 1882. Subsequently, treaties were signed with Britain, Italy, Russia, Germany and France.

6 The export tariff fixed by the Nanjing and Tianjin treaties (1842, 1860) amounted to the pre-Opium War rate of 2.5 *taels* per picul (or 5% ad valorem of an average price of 50 *taels* per picul). Since tea prices rarely reached that price level thereafter, tea continued to be taxed at a higher rate than intended. R.Gardella, *Harvesting Mountains*, p.95.

7 In 1866 China imported 141.9 million yards of cotton goods. By 1886 the total was 347.7 million yards. The average annual import of Indian opium increased from 75,000 chests in the 1860s to 82,000 chests in the 1870s. J.Ch'en, *State Economic Policies of the Ch'ing Government 1840-1895*, p.66.

8 In 1860 the post of Commissioner of Trade for the Northern Ports was created to parallel the existing commissionership for the Southern Ports. On becoming Governor-general of Zhili in 1870, Li Hongzhang was concurrently appointed Trade Commissioner for the Northern Ports. He subsequently took over many of the functions that would normally have been performed by the Zongli Yamen.

9 Ma is referring to the Shanghai Cotton Cloth Mill, formally established in 1882. By 1890 35,000 spindles and 350 looms were in operation. In 1892 it produced 4 million yards of cotton cloth and 1 million yards of cotton yarn. The mill was destroyed by fire in 1893. A.Feuerwerker, *China's Early Industrialization: Sheng Hsuan-huai and Mandarin Enterprise*, pp.208-217.

10 *jiu niu zhi yi mao*: lit: 'a single hair from nine oxhides'.

11 Ma uses the phrase *shouhui liquan* (regaining of economic rights), a key concept in reformist thought at this time.

12 *jiuquan* lit: 'the nine layers of hell', a Buddhist term.

13 The Chinese for San Francisco and Melbourne is *jiujinshan* (old gold mountain) and *xinjinshan* (new gold mountain) respectively.

14 Ming Dynasty (1368-1644).

15 This is a reference to Governor-general Zhang Zhidong's proposal of 1889.

16 Zhangbaishan is located in Jilin province.

17 Taishan (in Shandong province) is one of China's five sacred mountains.

18 The Mohe Gold Mine (along the Amur River) was opened in 1887.

19 Ninghai and Zhaoyuan are in Shandong province.

20 Pingdu is in Shandong province.

21 Before 1895 Kaiping was the only truly modern mine, using mechanical winding and pumps, and cages and guide rails in the shafts. T.Wright, *Coal Mining in China's Economy and Society 1895-1937* (Cambridge, Mass., 1984), p.37. It should be noted, however, that coal mining had been going on since the 1st century A.D. Coal pits in the 12th century were as large as those in 17th century Europe. The use of coal, however, was small on a per capita basis. Thus 17th century England (population 5 million) used as much coal as mid-19th century China with a population eighty times more in number. T.Wright, *ibid.*, p.9. Production at Kaiping, which got underway in 1881, increased from 3,613 tons to 75,317 tons in 1883. E.Carlson, *The Kaiping Mines 1877-1912*, p.13. By 1889 the mine was producing 247,867 tons and the company was also involved in gold mining in the north-east. The Kaiping Coal Mine Company planned to raise 800,000 *taels* of share capital, and by 1882 had received 1 million *taels* of paid up capital (although it still needed the assistance of government loans). The company did not pay any dividends on shares during the first ten years, the first dividend being paid in 1888. E.Carlson, *ibid.*, p.39. In 1900-1901, amidst the disorders of the Boxer uprising, the Kaiping company was taken over by an Anglo-Belgian corporation in which British investors gained a majority ownership.

22 *gong kui yi kui* lit: 'fail to build a mound for want of one final basket of earth'. The expression comes from the *Shangshu* (Book of History) in which the Duke of Shao advises King Wu: 'If you do not attend jealously to your small actions, the result will be to affect your virtue in great matters. In raising a mound of nine fathoms, the work may be unfinished for want of one basket of earth'. See C.Waltham, *Shu Ching: Book of History* (London, 1971), p.133.

23 The term Ma uses is *gongsi* (public company).

24 The expression used is *gaizao tuhao* (lit: 'to transform/remould local products').

Index

Index

ideas on silk and tea production, 90-92

in France, 14, 16, 17, 19, 20, 38-44, 46(fn.22)

influence of, 27-28

promotion of manufacturing and mining, 26-27, 94-100

merchants, 9, 10, 12, 13, 16, 25, 28

mining, 2, 5, 8, 11, 13, 16, 18, 95-100, 105(fn.21)

modernization, 1, 2, 7, 8, 9, 10, 11, 30(fn.22)

mufu, 12-13, 16

nationalism, 10, 11, 12, 13, 15, 27, 33(fn.50), 72(fn.16)

Opium War, 1, 72(fn.17), 104(fn.6)

Paris Exhibition (1878), 18, 20, 42-44, 46(fn.7,fn.8)

Qing dynasty, 1, 3, 4, 8, 11, 87(fn.3,fn.4,fn.5,fn.7), 104(fn.2,fn.3)

railroads, 2, 8, 10, 11, 13, 17, 18, 21-24, 35(fn.88,fn.89,fn.90), 96

reformist thought, 5, 6, 9-10, 12, 15, 16, 19, 20, 27, 72(fn.13), 104(fn.11)

Self-Strengthening Movement, 1-4, 7,
10, 11, 27, 29(fn.2,fn.4)

Shanghai Cotton Cloth Mill, 2, 6, 26-27, 104(fn.9)

Shen Baozhen, 10-11, 13, 21, 31(fn.36), 32(fn.38)

silk trade, 8, 9, 24-25, 26, 28, 31(fn.28), 36(fn.107), 90-91

Sino-Japanese War (1894-95), 2

Taiping Rebellion, 1, 5, 11, 26, 29(fn.1), 30(fn.25)

taxation, 2, 9, 10, 26, 28, 104(fn.3)

tea trade, 8-9, 24, 25, 26, 28, 36(fn.98), 90, 91, 92

Tongwenguan, 2, 46(fn.4), 52, 55-56(fn.12)

Tongzhi, Emepror, 4, 5, 96

Tongzhi Restoration, 5, 29(fn.2)

treaty ports, 1, 8, 12, 23, 28, 79

unequal treaties, 1, 8, 10

Wang Tao, 16, 17

Wudi, Emperor, 51, 55(fn.9)

Xue Fucheng, 16, 17, 34(fn.72,fn.73)

Zhang Zhidong, 2-3, 6, 22, 27, 105(fn.15)

Zongli Yamen, 2, 53, 54, 56(fn.13), 93

For Product Safety Concerns and Information please contact our EU
representative GPSR@taylorandfrancis.com
Taylor & Francis Verlag GmbH, Kaufingerstraße 24, 80331 München, Germany

www.ingramcontent.com/pod-product-compliance
Lightning Source LLC
Chambersburg PA
CBHW050525280326
41932CB00014B/2467

9 781138 983014